THE MASTER
OF MEN

THE MASTER OF MEN

Quotable Poems About Jesus

COMPILED BY

THOMAS CURTIS CLARK

Granger Index Reprint Series

BOOKS FOR LIBRARIES PRESS
FREEPORT, NEW YORK

STANDARD BOOK NUMBER:
8369-6137-4

LIBRARY OF CONGRESS CATALOG CARD NUMBER:
72-116396

MANUFACTURED
BY
HALLMARK LITHOGRAPHERS, INC.
IN THE U.S.A.

DEDICATED TO THE

MEMORY OF

MY FATHER

FOR FORTY-FIVE YEARS A MINISTER OF

THE GOSPEL OF CHRIST

CONTENTS

I

"THE WORLD SITS AT THE FEET OF CHRIST"

"THE WORLD SITS AT THE FEET OF CHRIST"

The world sits at the feet of Christ,
    Unknowing, blind, and unconsoled;
    It yet shall touch His garment's fold,
And feel the heavenly Alchemist
    Transform its very dust to gold.

From The Overheart   JOHN GREENLEAF WHITTIER

STRONG SON OF GOD

Strong Son of God, immortal Love,
Whom we, that have not seen Thy face,
By faith, and faith alone, embrace,
Believing where we cannot prove:

Thine are these orbs of light and shade;
Thou madest Life, in man and brute;
Thou madest Death,—and lo, Thy foot
Is on the skull which Thou hast made.

Thou wilt not leave us in the dust:
Thou madest man, he knows not why,—
He thinks he was not made to die;
And Thou hast made him: Thou art just.

3

Thou seemest human and divine,—
The highest, holiest manhood, Thou:
Our wills are ours, we know not how;
Our wills are ours, to make them Thine.

From In Memoriam   ALFRED TENNYSON

THOU CRYSTAL CHRIST

But Thee, but Thee, O sovereign Seer of Time,
But Thee, O poet's Poet, Wisdom's Tongue,
But Thee, O man's best Man, O love's best Love,
O perfect life in perfect labor writ,
O all men's Comrade, Servant, King, or Priest—
What *if* or *yet,* what mole, what flaw, what lapse,
What least defect or shadow of defect,
What rumor, tattled by an enemy,
Of inference loose, what lack of grace
Even in torture's grasp, or sleep's, or death's—
Oh, what amiss may I forgive in Thee,
Jesus, good Paragon, thou Crystal Christ?

From The Crystal   SIDNEY LANIER

THE BETTER PART

Long fed on boundless hopes, O race of man,
How angrily thou spurn'st all simpler fare!
"Christ," some one says, "was human as we **are;**
No judge eyes us from heaven, our sin to scan;

We live no more, when we have done our span."
"Well, then, for Christ," thou answerest, "who can care?
From sin which Heaven records not, why forbear?
Live we like brutes our life without a plan!"

So answerest thou; but why not rather say,—
"Hath man no second life? *Pitch this one high!*
Sits there no judge in heaven, our sin to see?
More strictly, then, the inward judge obey!
Was Christ a man like us? *Ah! let us try*
If we then, too, can be such men as He!"

MATTHEW ARNOLD

THE ETERNAL WORD

In the beginning was the Word;
    Athwart the Chaos, night:
It gleamed with quick creative power
    And there was life and light.

Thy Word, O God, is living yet
    Amid earth's restless strife,
New harmony creating still
    And ever higher life.

O Word that broke the stillness first,
    Sound on, and never cease
Till all earth's darkness be made light,
    And all her discord peace.

Till selfish passion, strife and wrong,
   Thy summons shall have heard,
And Thy creation be complete,
   O Thou Eternal Word.

HENRY WADSWORTH LONGFELLOW

From OUR MASTER

We may not climb the heavenly steeps
   To bring the Lord Christ down;
In vain we search the lowest deeps,
   For Him no depths can drown.

But warm, sweet, tender, even yet
   A present help is He;
And faith has still its Olivet
   And love its Galilee.

The healing of His seamless dress
   Is by our beds of pain;
We touch Him in life's throng and press,
   And we are whole again.

Through Him the first fond prayers are said
   Our lips of childhood frame;
The last low whispers of the dead
   Are burdened with His name.

O Lord and Master of us all!
   Whate'er our name or sign,
We own Thy sway, we hear Thy call
   We test our lives by Thine.

JOHN GREENLEAF WHITTIER

THE FACE OF JESUS CHRIST

Is this the face that thrills with awe
    Seraphs who veil their face above?
Is this the face without a flaw,
    The face that is the face of love?
Yea, this defaced, a lifeless clod,
    Hath all creation's love sufficed,
Hath satisfied the love of God,
    This face, the face of Jesus Christ.

From The Descent from the Cross   CHRISTINA ROSSETTI

TO AND FRO ABOUT THE CITY

Shakespeare is dust, and will not come
To question from his Avon tomb,
And Socrates and Shelley keep
An Attic and Italian sleep.

They will not see us, nor again
Shall indignation light the brain
Where Lincoln on his woodland height
Tells out the spring and winter night.

They see not. But, O Christians, who
Throng Holborn and Fifth Avenue,
May you not meet, in spite of death,
A traveler from Nazareth?

         JOHN DRINKWATER

OUR DIVINEST SYMBOL

Look on our divinest Symbol—on Jesus of Nazareth!
Higher has human thought not yet reached.

Sublimer in this world I know nothing than a peasant-saint;
could such now anywhere be met with? Such a one will
take thee back to Nazareth itself; thou wilt see the splen-
dor of heaven spring forth from the humblest depths of
earth, like a light shining in great darkness.

Our highest Orpheus walked in Judea eighteen hundred
years ago; his sphere-melody flowing in wild native tones
took captive the ravished souls of men; and, being of a
truth sphere-melody, still flows and sounds, though now
with thousandfold accompaniments and rich symphonies,
through all our hearts; and modulates and divinely leads
them.

THOMAS CARLYLE

TO ONE ALONE

To One alone my thoughts arise,
The Eternal Truth, the Good and Wise,
To Him I cry,
Who shared on earth our common lot,
But the world comprehended not
His deity.

From Coplas de Manrique   HENRY WADSWORTH LONGFELLOW

COME UNTO ME

We labor and are heavy-laden. Where
Shall we find rest unto our souls? We bleed
On thorn and flint, and rove in pilgrim weed
From shrine to shrine, but comfort is not there.
What went we out into thy desert bare,
O Human Life, to see? Thy greenest reed
Is Love, unmighty for our utmost need,
And shaken with the wind of our despair.
A voice from Heaven like dew on Hermon falleth,
That voice whose passion paled the olive leaf
In thy dusky aisles, Gethsemane, thou blest
Of gardens. 'Tis the Man of Sorrows calleth,
The Man of Sorrows and acquaint with grief:
"Come unto Me, and I will give you rest."

KATHARINE LEE BATES

THE SONG OF A HEATHEN

If Jesus Christ is a man—
    And only a man—I say
That of all mankind I cleave to Him
    And to Him will I cleave alway.

If Jesus Christ is a god—
    And the only God—I swear
I will follow Him through heaven and hell,
    The earth, the sea, and the air!

RICHARD WATSON GILDER

THE MAN CHRIST

He built no temple, yet the farthest sea
Can yield no shore that's barren of His place
　　For bended knee.

He wrote no book, and yet His words and prayer
Are intimate on many myriad tongues,
　　Are counsel everywhere.

The life He lived has never been assailed,
Nor any precept, as He lived it, yet
　　Has ever failed.

He built no kingdom, yet a King from youth
He reigned, is reigning yet; they call His realm
　　The kingdom of the Truth.

THERESE LINDSEY

CHRIST'S REIGN OF PEACE

And He shall charm and soothe, and breathe and bless,
The roaring of war shall cease upon the air,
Falling of tears and all the voices of sorrow,
And He shall take the terror from the grave.

And He shall still that old sob of the sea,
And heal the unhappy fancies of the wind,
And turn the moon from all that hopeless quest;
Trees without care shall blossom, and all the fields
Shall without labor unto harvest come.

STEPHEN PHILLIPS

THAT ONE FACE

That one Face, far from vanish, rather grows,
Or decomposes but to recompose,
Become my Universe that feels and knows.

From The Epilogue   ROBERT BROWNING

"LORD OF MY HEART'S ELATION"

Lord of my heart's elation,
  Spirit of things unseen,
Be Thou my aspiration
  Consuming and serene!

Bear up, bear out, bear onward,
  This mortal soul alone,
To selfhood or oblivion,
  Incredibly Thine own,

As the foamheads are loosened
  And blown along the sea,
Or sink and merge forever
  In that which bids them be.

I, too, must climb in wonder,
  Uplift at Thy command,—
Be one with my frail fellows
  Beneath the wind's strong hand.

A fleet and shadowy column
  Of dust or mountain rain,
To walk the earth a moment
  And be dissolved again.

Be Thou my exaltation
   Or fortitude of mien,
Lord of the world's elation,
   Thou breath of things unseen!

BLISS CARMAN

AND SO THE WORD HAD BREATH

Though truths in manhood darkly join
Deep-seated in our mystic frame,
We yield all blessing to the name
Of Him that made them current coin;

For Wisdom dealt with mortal powers
Where truth in closest words shall fail,
When truth embodied in a tale
Shall enter in at lowly doors.

And so the Word had breath and wrought
With human hands the creed of creeds
In loveliness of perfect deeds,
More strong than all poetic thought;

Which he may read that binds the sheaf
Or builds the house, or digs the grave,
And those wild eyes that watch the wave
In roarings round the coral reef.

From In Memoriam   ALFRED TENNYSON

GOD IN CHRIST

I say the acknowledgment of God in Christ
Accepted by thy reason, solves for thee
All questions in the world and out of it.

From Death in the Desert   ROBERT BROWNING

I AM THE WAY

Thou art the Way.
Hadst Thou been nothing but the goal,
    I cannot say
If Thou hadst ever met my soul.

    I cannot see—
I, child of process—if there lies
    An end for me,
Full of repose, full of replies.

    I'll not reproach
The road that winds, my feet that err,
    Access, Approach
Art Thou, Time, Way, Wayfarer.

ALICE MEYNELL

"THE HOLIEST AMONG THE MIGHTY"

Christ who, being the holiest among the mighty, and the
mightiest among the holy, lifted with His pierced hands
empires off their hinges and turned the stream of cen-
turies out of its channel, and still governs the ages.

JEAN PAUL RICHTER

A CREED

Here is the Truth in a little creed,
  Enough for all the roads we go:
In Love is all the law we need,
  In Christ is all the God we know.

EDWIN MARKHAM

ONE THERE WAS

One there was Who, passing by,
Touched all life with alchemy,
Grass of field or birds of air
Made His heart of God aware.
Of common salt or smooth-worn yoke
A figure patterned for eager folk;
Of wayside spring or granary
Symbols He made which never die;
From mustard seed or branching vine,
Similitudes of things divine.
Meaning to leavening dough He lent;
He made, of bread, a sacrament.

STELLA FISHER BURGESS

THE REAL CHRIST

Behold Him now as He comes!
  Not the Christ of our subtle creeds,
But the Light of our hearts and our homes,
  Our hopes, our fears, our needs,

The brother of want and blame,
  The lover of women and men,
With a love that puts to shame
  All passions of mortal ken. . . .

Ah, no, thou life of the heart,
  Never shalt thou depart!
Not till the heaven of God
  Shall lighten each human clod;
Not till the world shall climb
  To the height serene, sublime,
Shall the Christ who enters our door
  Pass to return no more.

From The Passing Christ   Richard Watson Gilder

FINDING THE WAY

Never in a costly palace did I rest on golden bed,
Never in a hermit's cavern have I eaten idle bread.

Born within a lowly stable where the cattle round Me
  stood,
Trained a carpenter of Nazareth, I have toiled and found
  it good.

They who tread the path of labour follow where My feet
  have trod;
They who work without complaining do the Holy will of
  God.

Where the many toil together, there am I among My own;
When the tirèd workman sleepeth, then am I with him
  alone.

I, the Peace that passeth knowledge, dwell amid the daily
  strife,
I, the Bread of Heaven, am broken in the sacrament of
  life.

HENRY VAN DYKE

HIS LAUREATE

Before Christ left the Citadel of Light,
To tread the dreadful way of human birth,
His shadow sometimes fell upon the earth
And those who saw it wept with joy and fright.
"Thou art Apollo, than the sun more bright!"
They cried, "Our music is of little worth,
But thrill our blood with thy creative mirth
Thou god of song, thou lord of lyric might!"

O singing pilgrim! who could love and follow
Your lover Christ, through even love's despair,
You knew within the cypress-darkened hollow
The feet that on the mountain are so fair.
For it was Christ that was your own Apollo,
And thorns were in the laurel on your hair.

JOYCE KILMER

THE ONE GREAT WORD

Christ—the one great word
Well worth all languages in earth or Heaven.

SAMUEL BAILEY

THE PATH OF THE STARS

Down through the spheres there came the Name of One
Who is the Law of Beauty and of Light;
He came, and as He came the waiting Night
Shook with gladness of a Day begun;
And as He came, He said: "Thy Will be Done
On Earth"; and all His vibrant words were white
And glistening with silver, and their might
Was of the glory of a rising sun.
Unto the Stars sang out His Living Words
White and with silver, and their rhythmic sound
Was a mighty symphony unfurled;
And back from out the Stars like homing birds
They fell in love upon the sleeping ground
And were forever in a wakened world.

THOMAS S. JONES, JR.

SEE THE CHRIST STAND!

"I believe it! 'Tis Thou, God, that givest, 'tis I who receive:
In the first is the last, in Thy will is my power to believe.
All's one gift: Thou canst grant it, moreover, as prompt
to my prayer
As I breathe out this breath, as I open these arms to the
air.
From Thy will stream the worlds, life and nature, Thy
dread Sabaoth:
I will?—the mere atoms despise me! Why am I not loth
To look that, even that, in the face too? Why is it I dare
Think but lightly of such impuissance? What stops my
despair?

This:—'tis not what man Does which exalts him, but
what man Would do!

See the King—I would help him but cannot, the wishes
fall through.

Could I wrestle to raise him from sorrow, grow poor to
enrich,—

To fill up His life, starve my own out,—I would; know-
ing which,

I know that my service is perfect. Oh, speak through me
now!

Would I suffer for Him that I love? So wouldst Thou—
so wilt Thou!

So shall crown Thee the topmost, ineffablest, uttermost
crown—

And Thy love fill infinitude wholly, nor leave up nor
down,

One spot for the creature to stand in! It is by no breath,

Turn of eye, wave of hand, that salvation joins issue with
death!

As Thy Love is discovered almighty, almighty he proved

Thy power, that exists with and for it, of being Beloved!

He who did most, shall bear most: the strongest shall
stand the most weak.

'Tis the weakness in strength, that I cry for! my flesh, that
I seek

In the Godhead! I seek and I find it. O Saul, it shall be

A Face like my face that receives thee; a Man like to me,

Thou shalt love and be loved by, forever: a Hand like this
hand

Shall throw open the gates of new life to thee! See the
Christ stand!"

From Saul   ROBERT BROWNING

THE TRUE NEED

But this: to know Thy life, without a stain.
I do not wish to see my sins more plain,

I would not see the vileness of my heart,
But this would know: how pure and true Thou art.

I would forget my paltry life, so small,
And know Thy greatness, Thou, my All in All.

Oh! teach me not how deep my spirit's night,
But flood me with Thy beams, Thou Perfect Light!

THOMAS CURTIS CLARK

THE CAPTAINS OF THE YEARS

I watched the Captains
    A-riding, riding
    Down the years;
The men of mystic grip
    Of soul, a-riding
Between a hedge of spears.

I saw their banners
    A-floating, floating
    Over all,
Till each of them had passed,
    And Christ came riding
A donkey lean and small.

I watched the Captains
　A-turning, staring,
　　Proud and set,
At Christ a-riding there—
　So calmly riding
The Road men can't forget.

I watched the Captains
　Dismounting, waiting—
　　None now led—
The Captains bowing low!
　The Caesars waiting!
While Christ rode on ahead.

ARTHUR R. MACDOUGALL, JR.

THE GREAT WAGER

How is it proved?
It isn't proved, you fool; it can't be proved.
How can you prove a victory before
It's won? How can you prove a man who leads
To be a leader worth the following,
Unless you follow to the death, and out
Beyond mere death, which is not anything
But Satan's lie upon eternal life?
Well—God's my leader, and I hold that He
Is good, and strong enough to work His plan
And purpose out to its appointed end.

I walk in crowded streets, where men
And women, mad with lust, loose-lipped, and lewd,

Go promenading down to hell's wide gates;
Yet have I looked into my mother's eyes
And seen the light that never was on sea
Or land, the light of love, pure love and true,
And on that love I bet my life. . . .

. . . . I bet my life on beauty, truth,
And love! not abstract, but incarnate truth;
Not beauty's passing shadow, but its self,
Its very self made flesh—love realized.
I bet my life on Christ, Christ crucified.

G. A. STUDDERT KENNEDY

OUR CHRIST

In Christ I feel the heart of God
    Throbbing from heaven through earth;
Life stirs again within the clod,
    Renewed in beauteous birth;
The soul springs up, a flower of prayer,
Breathing His breath out on the air.

In Christ I touch the hand of God,
    From His pure Height reached down,
By blessed ways before untrod,
    To lift us to our crown;
Victory that only perfect is
Through loving sacrifice, like His.

Holding His hand, my steadied feet
    May walk the air, the seas;

On life and death His smile falls sweet,
   Lights up all mysteries;
Stranger nor exile can I be
In new worlds where He leadeth me.

LUCY LARCOM

CREDO

Not what, but Whom, I do believe!
   That, in my darkest hour of need,
   Hath comfort that no mortal creed
   To mortal man may give.
Not what, but Whom!
   For Christ is more than all the creeds,
   And His full life of gentle deeds
   Shall all the creeds outlive.
Not what I do believe, but Whom!
   Who walks beside me in the gloom?
   Who shares the burden wearisome?
   Who all the dim way doth illume,
   And bids me look beyond the tomb
   The larger life to live?
Not what I do believe, but Whom!
Not what, but Whom!

JOHN OXENHAM

NOT THOU FROM US!

Not Thou from us, O Lord, but we
Withdraw ourselves from Thee.

When we are dark and dead,
And Thou art covered with a cloud,
Hanging before Thee, like a shroud,
So that our prayer can find no way,
Oh! teach us that we do not say,
  "Where is *Thy* brightness fled?"

But that we search and try
What in ourselves has wrought this blame;
For Thou remainest still the same,
But earth's own vapors earth may fill
With darkness and thick clouds, while still
  The sun is in the sky.

RICHARD CHENEVIX TRENCH

THE DEATHLESS TALE

Had He not breathed His breath
Truly at Nazareth;
Had not His very feet
Roamed many a hill and street;
Had Mary's story gone
To Time's oblivion;
Had the sweet record paled
And the truth not prevailed;
Dormant and bleak had been
This transitory scene,
And dark, thrice dark our earth
Unknowing of His birth.

The flowers beheld His face,
The stars knew His white grace.

The grass was greener for
His humble stable door;
The rose upon its stem
Redder for Bethlehem.
And we—are we not wise
To cling with avid eyes
To the old tale, and be
Moved by its memory?
Unutterably dim
Our bright world, lacking Him.

CHARLES HANSON TOWNE

IN THE LANES OF NAZARETH

He sang, too,
    In the lanes of Nazareth,
With sunlit eyes and boyish voice,
    Quickly out of breath.

He dreamed, too,
    Of mountains and a city,
Where men would trample gems
    And treasure pity.

He loved, too,
    But some way friends forgot,
When swords and staves and kisses
    Cut the lover's knot.

He grieved, too,
    For all His songs unsung.
They gave Him vinegar for songs
    Upon a parching tongue.

He sighed, too,
    With quickly-failing breath,
For souls and songs and little lanes
    In Nazareth.

EARL MARLATT

THE WILDERNESS

Up from the Jordan straight His way He took
To that lone wilderness, where rocks are hurled,
And strewn, and piled—as if the ancient world
In strong convulsions seethed and writhed and shook,
Which heaved the valleys up, and sunk each brook,
And flung the molten rock like ribbons curled
In midst of gray around the mountains whirled:—
A grim land, of a fierce, forbidding look.
The wild beasts haunt its barren stony heights,
And wilder visions came to tempt Him there;
For forty days and forty weary nights,
Alone He faced His mortal self and sin,
Chaos without, and chaos reigned within,
Subdued and conquered by the might of prayer.

CAROLINE HAZARD

TEMPTED

Into the wilderness
Straightway our Lord was driven of the Spirit;
Swept by that stress
Of rapture, sun and stars were but one shining
Till forty days had passed
And, Son of Man though Son of God, He hungered.

Why should He fast
With power to make stones bread; why fear, with succor
Of angels at His call;
Why fail, when all the world was to His Father
A golden ball,
One out of many, but a little present
For a beloved Son?

Ecstasy, faint with its own bliss, encountered
The scorpion
Of self, love's enemy. For love is holy
In loving; love is safe
Only in saving; love, despised, rejected,
The world's white waif,
Needs nothing that this earth can give of glory,
For love dwelleth in God.

So Christ's immortal rose above His mortal
And on it trod.

KATHARINE LEE BATES

TEMPTATION

They took Him to a mountain-top to see
Where earth's fair kingdoms flung their golden net
To snare the feet and trick the souls of men.
With slimy craft and cynic guile they said:
If He but sees the glory and the pride,
The pomps and pleasures of this tinsel world,
He will forget His splendid futile dreams.
And so they took Him up and tempted Him.

They pointed far across their level earth,
East to the fabled empires of the Ind,
Whose rulers' power was as the power of gods,
Where caravans with tinkling camel-bells
Brought silks and perfumes, pearls and ivory,
And tribute from far humbled provinces;
South to the magic kingdom of the Nile,
To Nubia and Abyssinia,
Jungle and desert kingdoms, rude but rich
With slaves and gems and golden yellow sands;
Northward to barbarous lands but dimly seen,
Savage but surging with unmeasured strength;
West where Rome's empire sent her legions forth,
Conquering, building, ruling with wise force,
The mighty mother of an unborn brood
Of nations which should rise and rule the world.

All this they spread before Him, tempting Him,
And watched to see ambition light His eye,
The lust of power darken His bright face,
And avarice crook His hands to clutch the gold.

But from the mountain peak He raised His eyes,
And saw the deep, calm sky, the stars, and God.

WINFRED ERNEST GARRISON

BY THE SEA OF GALILEE

Erect in youthful grace and radiant
   With spirit forces, all imparadised
In a divine compassion, down the slant
   Of these remembering hills He came, the Christ.

KATHARINE LEE BATES

A FISHERMAN SPEAKS
(Anno Domini, 33)

Oh, He who walked with fishermen
  Was man of men in Galilee;
He told us endless wonder-tales,
  His laugh was hale and free.

The water changed He into wine
  To please a poor man's company;
I saw Him walk one wretched night
  Upon a troubled sea.

And when the rabble cried for blood,
  I saw Him nailed upon a tree;
He showed how a brave man could die;
  The Prince of men was He.

And rough men, we, who never wept,
  Wept when they nailed Him to the tree;
Oh, He was more than man, Who walked
  With us in Galilee.

SCHARMEL IRIS

THE TEACHER

He sent men out to preach the living Word,
  Aflame with all the ardor of His fire;
They spoke the Truth, wherever truth. was heard
  But back to Him they brought their hearts'-desire;

They turned to Him through all the lengthening days
  With each perplexity of life or creed.
His deep reward, not that they spoke His praise,
  But that they brought to Him their human need.

HILDEGARDE HOYT SWIFT

BLIND BARTIMEUS

Blind Bartimeus at the gates
Of Jericho in darkness waits;
He hears the crowd—he hears a breath
Say, "It is Christ of Nazareth!"
And calls in tones of agony,
"Jesus, have mercy now on me!"

The thronging multitudes increase;
Blind Bartimeus, hold thy peace!
But still, above the noisy crowd,
The beggar's cry is shrill and loud;
Until they say, "He calleth thee!"
"Fear not, arise, He calleth thee!"

Then saith the Christ, as silent stands
The crowd, "What wilt thou at My hands?"
And he replies, "O give me light!
Rabbi, restore the blind man's sight."
And Jesus answers,
                          "Go in peace
Thy faith from blindness gives release!"

Ye that have eyes yet cannot see,
In darkness and in misery,

Recall those mighty Voices Three,
"Jesus, have mercy now on me!
Fear not, arise, and go in peace!
Thy faith from blindness gives release!"

HENRY WADSWORTH LONGFELLOW

CONTRAST

What wrote He on the parched and dusty ground
When men brought to Him one condemned in sin
Whose life an ugly, tangled web had been?
The sneering mob stalked haughtily around
And mocked the woman, while the clamorous sound
Of raucous voices grew into a din
That shrieked and cursed at her and all her kin,
As she in silence stood, with terror bound.

They faced each other—He, the Stainless One,
And she—the harlot—vilely sick within.
The brutes who brought her, by His will outdone,
Each one, himself, perchance, a libertine,
Slunk off, and left them standing there alone,
And, at His word, she rose up, white and clean.

AUBERT EDGAR BRUCE

ALONE INTO THE MOUNTAIN

All day from that deep well of life within
Himself has He drawn healing for the press
Of folk, restoring strength, forgiving sin,
Quieting frenzy, comforting distress.

Shadows of evening fall, yet wildly still
They throng Him, touch Him, clutch His garment's hem,
Fall down and clasp His feet, cry on Him, till
The Master, spent, slips from the midst of them
And climbs the mountain for a cup of peace,
Taking a sheer and rugged track untrod
Save by a poor lost sheep with thorn-torn fleece
That follows on and hears Him talk with God.

KATHARINE LEE BATES

ON SYRIAN HILLS

It is said the Bedouins cry, on the Syrian hills, a clear
Loud summons to War, and the tribes far distant hearken
    and hear,
So wondrous rare is the air, so crystal the atmosphere.
Their call is to arms; but One, in the centuries long ago,
Spake there for Peace, in tones that were marvellous sweet
    and low,
And the ages they hear Him yet, and His voice do the
    nations know.

RICHARD BURTON

IN HIS STEPS

Should not the glowing lilies of the field
    With keener splendor mark His footsteps yet—
Prints of the gentle feet Whose passing healed
    All blight from Tabor unto Olivet?

KATHARINE LEE BATES

A BALLAD OF TREES AND THE MASTER

Into the woods my Master went,
Clean forspent.
Into the woods my Master came,
Forspent with love and shame.
But the olives they were not blind to Him,
The thorn-tree had a mind to Him,
When into the woods He came.

Out of the woods my Master went,
And He was well content.
Out of the woods my Master came,
Content with death and shame.
When Death and Shame would woo Him last,
From under the trees they drew Him last:
'Twas on a tree they slew Him—last
When out of the woods He came.

SIDNEY LANIER

AVE MARIA GRATIA PLENA

Was this His coming! I had hoped to see
A scene of wondrous glory, as was told
Of some great God who in a rain of gold
Broke open bars and fell on Danaë:
Or a dread vision as when Semele,
Sickening for love and unappeased desire,
Prayed to see God's clear body, and the fire
Caught her brown limbs and slew her utterly.
With such glad dreams I sought this holy place,

And now with wondering eyes and heart I stand
Before this supreme mystery of Love:
Some kneeling girl with passionless pale face,
An angel with a lily in his hand,
And over both the white wings of a Dove.

OSCAR WILDE

MIRACLE

Oh, paltry miracles
 That satisfy
The heart: emollient clay
 On blinded eye;

The mortal foot that walked
 Upon the wave,
The meager fish and loaf
 Of bread I gave!

Oh, darkly seeing eyes
 That praise and damn,
Blind to the miracle:
 I love . . . I am.

EDITH MIRICK

TO HIM ALL LIFE WAS BEAUTY

To Him all life was Beauty. The sun upon the hills,
The sweeping shadows, and the winding lane.
Morning He loved, with dewdrops on the flowers;
Evening, with sunset and soft, warm April rain.

Friends He found in lepers stumbling to Him,
Love in those who hate, grace in sinners' eyes.
Dawn He saw with all earth's new-born glory,
Twilight and darkness, and hope in human sighs.
Youth was His, and springtime, and music in the trees;
Life was His, and sunshine, and the murmuring of the bees.
Joy in healing broken hearts; manhood's noble strife;
All the wonder and the beauty of a sacred human life.

. . . . .

He walked the common lanes, the city streets He trod,
And in His heart was Beauty . . . the Beauty born of God.

A. L. C.

THE BRONZE CHRIST

Love, love was the creed that He taught,
　　And peace, perfect peace, everywhere;
The past that is dead is as naught,
　　The present and future are fair.
Could we but see over the tomb
　　The flowers of Christ's tenderness bloom,
Grand, grand were the ages to come,
　　For the voices of strife would be dumb!

CLINTON SCOLLARD

HIS NAME

He did not come to judge the world, He did not come to
　　blame;
He did not only come to seek—it was to save He came:
And when we call Him Savior, then we call Him by His
　　name.

From Songs of Salvation　　　　　　　　DORA GREENWELL

HE, TOO, LOVED BEAUTY

I who love beauty in the open valleys,
  Tintings of sunset, and the swallow's flight,
Must breathe the air of squalid city alleys,
  Shut from the cool caresses of the night.
Wistful of fragrance where the springtime dallies,
  Sharing with sordid souls a city's blight.

He, too, loved beauty, but a city drew Him.
  Flowers He found in little children's eyes;
Something of grace in lepers stumbling to Him;
  Fragrance from spikenard split in sweet surprise;
Joy in forgiving men at last who slew Him;
  Courage in service, hope in sacrifice.

                              E. McNeill Poteat, Jr.

THE CONQUERORS

I saw the Conquerors riding by
  With trampling feet of horse and men:
Empire on empire like the tide
  Flooded the world and ebbed again;

A thousand banners caught the sun,
  And cities smoked along the plain,
And laden down with silk and gold
  And heaped-up pillage groaned the wain.

I saw the Conquerors riding by,
  Splashing through loathsome floods of war—
The Crescent leaning o'er its hosts,
  And the barbaric scimitar—

And continents of moving spears,
  And storms of arrows in the sky,
And all the instruments sought out
  By cunning men that men may die!

I saw the Conquerors riding by
  With cruel lips and faces wan:
Musing on kingdoms sacked and burned
  There rode the Mongol Genghis Khan;

And Alexander, like a god,
  Who sought to weld the world in one;
And Cæsar with his laurel wreath;
  And like a thing from Hell the Hun;

And leading, like a star the van,
  Heedless of upstretched arm and groan,
Inscrutable Napoleon went
  Dreaming of empire, and alone . . .

Then all they perished from the earth
  As fleeting shadows from a glass,
And, conquering down the centuries,
  Came Christ, the Swordless, on an ass!

HARRY KEMP

IRONY OF GOD

In vain
They shook their garments;
He did not hear the tinkling
Of little bells
On priestly hems;
Nor smell the smoky savor
Of slaughtered, burning life.

He did not see Jerusalem—
Nor Rome;
He passed by all "best families"
To dwell at last in Nazareth,
With Mary,
Mother of that Son
Who fraternized with fishermen;
Found heaven in little children;
And had a friend
Named Mary Magdalene.

EVA WARNER

CHRIST AND THE PAGAN

I had no God but these,
The sacerdotal Trees,
And they uplifted me.
"I hung upon a tree."

The sun and moon I saw,
And reverential awe
Subdued me day and night.
"I am the perfect Light."

Within a lifeless Stone—
All other gods unknown—
I sought Divinity.
"The Corner-Stone am I."

For sacrificial feast,
I slaughtered man and beast,
Red recompense to gain.
"So I, a Lamb, was slain."

*"Yea; such My hungering Grace
That wheresoe'er My face
Is hidden, none may grope
Beyond eternal Hope."*

JOHN B. TABB

EVIDENCE

"Where is God!" inquired the mind:
"To His presence I am blind.
I can tell each blade of grass,
Read the tempests as they pass;
I have learned what metals lie
In the earth's deep mystery;
Every voice of field and wood
I have heard and understood;
Ancient secrets of the sea
Are no longer dark to me:
But the wonders of the earth
Bring no thought of God to birth."
Then the heart spake quietly,
"Hast thou thought of Calvary?"

"Where is God?" inquired the mind;
"To His presence I am blind.
I have scanned each star and sun,
Traced the certain course they run;
I have weighed them in my scale,
And can tell when each will fail;
From the caverns of the night
I have brought new worlds to light;
I have measured earth and sky,
Read each zone with steady eye;
But no sign of God appears
In the glory of the spheres."
But the heart spake wistfully,
"Hast thou looked on Calvary?"

THOMAS CURTIS CLARK

"STILL THOU ART QUESTION"

We place Thy sacred name upon our brows;
   Our cycles from Thy natal day we score:
Yet, spite of all our songs and all our vows,
   We thirst and ever thirst to know Thee more.

For Thou art Mystery and Question still;
   Even when we see Thee lifted as a sign
Drawing all men unto that hapless hill
   With the resistless power of Love Divine.

Still Thou art Question—while rings in our ears
   Thine outcry to a world discord-beset:
Have I been with thee all these many years,
   O World—dost thou not know Me even yet?

AUTHOR UNKNOWN

THE UNTRIED DOOR

Behold, we stand at many doors and knock;
From house to house we pass in the cold night!
But hear not any creaking of the lock
And through no crevice see the welcome light!

Silent those palaces for evermore!
Only one house remains untried, where stands
The Friend, Who waits our knocking on the door—
Upon the latch His scarred and eager hands.

EDWARD SHILLITO

II

THE WAY OF THE CROSS

THE CROWD

Always He feared you;
For you knew Him only as the man of loaves and fishes—
The man who did marvelous things:
He who raised Lazarus,
Healed the lame, and made the blind to see.
Fleeing from you, He sought the solace of the garden.

He must have known
That you would cry, "Release unto us Barabbas!"
And fling cruel words at Him
As He climbed to Golgotha alone,
Perhaps He knew
That some day you would build creeds about Him,
And lose Him in massive structures of stone,
With costly windows, dignified ritual, and eloquent
    preachers;
While, outside, He waited. . . .
Sad. . . . and alone.

IRENE MCKEIGHAN

RIDING THROUGH JERUSALEM

I thought it strange He asked for me,
    And bade me carry Him,
The noblest one of all the earth,
    Into Jerusalem!

43

But rumor goes He loved the meek
　And such on Him might call,
That may be why He trusted me
　The humblest beast of all.

Yet though He was so great and wise
　Unequaled in His might,
I scarcely knew I bore a King
　So light He rode—so light!

They sang Hosannah in the streets,
　But I have heard men say,
The only time they praised their King
　Was when He rode that day.

Men pushed and shouted all around,
　The air was thick with cries,
They spread their garments at my feet,
　And palms before mine eyes.

They strewed the narrow road with boughs
　And barred my path again—
But the tenderest hand I ever felt
　Was on my bridle chain.

MARION SUSAN CAMPBELL

WEDNESDAY IN HOLY WEEK

Man's life is death. Yet Christ endured to live,
　Preaching and teaching, toiling to and fro,
Few men accepting what He yearned to give,
　Few men with eyes to know
　His face, that Face of Love He stooped to show.

Man's death is life. For Christ endured to die
  In slow unuttered weariness of pain,
A curse and an astonishment, passed by,
  Pointed at, mocked again
  By men for whom He shed His blood—in vain?

CHRISTINA ROSSETTI

AT GETHSEMANE

There is a sighing in the pallid sprays
  Of these old olives, as if still they kept
Their pitying watch, in Nature's faithful ways,
  As on that night when the disciples slept.

KATHARINE LEE BATES

SONG

What trees were in Gethsemane,
  What flowers were there to scent,
When Christ for you, and Christ for me,
  Into His garden went?

The fragrant cedar tree was there,
  The lily pale and slim:
They saw His grief, they heard His prayer,
  And wept their dews for Him.

And that is why the cedars green
  And why the lilies white
Do whisper of the Master's love
  In gardens, late at night.

CHARLES G. BLANDEN

JUDAS

"And one that dips with me the sop."—"Not I!"
He rises from the quiet group he knew
Before the priestly court: "What will you buy?"
For thirty pieces he bought death for two.

HOWARD MCKINLEY CORNING

JUDAS ISCARIOT

The disciple wrapped close his garment of red
And far from Gethsemane garden fled.

Judas Iscariot looked at some land,
And fingered the blood-money held in his hand;

This would he buy and here would he live,
Gather his crops and—"Give, my son, give

"All that you have for the Kingdom of God";
Something that glittered fell on the sod.

It was not hard silver that lay shining there,
What! Can it be Judas ventures a prayer?

"Father, forgive me, oh, what have I done?
I have betrayed Him, my Master, Thy Son.

"He loved me, His face when He gave me the wine
Was saddened with grieving for sin that was mine.

"I have betrayed Him—oh, was it for this
That I sold my Master—sold, with a kiss!

"And shall I live while Jesus is slain?
Here is a rope. Quick, knot it again—"

* * *

Golgotha in darkness; and Judas alone
Waited the judgment before the white throne.

Through paths of tall lilies that bent left and right,
Christ came to heaven, clothed all in light.

While stars sang together to welcome the Son,
He heard but the moans of the sorrowing one.

His merciful eyes on the penitent head,—
"Father, forgive . . . he knew not," He said.

CATHERINE CATE COBLENTZ

GOOD FRIDAY

Peter and James and John,
The sad tale runneth on—
All slept and Thee forgot;
One said he knew Thee not.

Peter and James and John,
The sad tale runneth on—
I am that one, the three;
Thus have I done to Thee.

Under a garden wall,
I lay at evenfall;
I waked. Thou calledst me;
I had not watched with Thee.

Peter and James and John,
The sad tale runneth on—
By the priest's fagot hot,
I said I knew Thee not.

The little maid spake out:
"With Him thou wentest about."
"This Man I never met—"
I hear the cock crow yet.

LIZETTE WOODWORTH REESE

"THE LORD TURNED, AND LOOKED UPON PETER"

The Savior looked on Peter. Ay, no word,
No gesture of reproach! the heavens serene,
Though heavy with armed justice, did not lean
Their thunders that way! the forsaken Lord
Looked only on the traitor. None record
What that look was, none guess: for those who have seen
Wronged lovers loving through a death-pang keen,
Or pale-cheeked martyrs smiling to a sword,
Have missed Jehovah at the judgment-call.
And Peter, from the height of blasphemy—
"I never knew this man"—did quail and fall,
As knowing straight that God—and turned free
And went out speechless from the face of all,
And filled the silence, weeping bitterly.

ELIZABETH BARRETT BROWNING

QUO VADIS?

Peter, outworn,
And menaced by the sword,
Shook off the dust of Rome;
And, as he fled,
Met One, with eager face,
Hastening cityward,
And, to his vast amaze,
It was the Lord.

"Lord, whither goest Thou?"
He cried, importunate,
And Christ replied,—
  "Peter, I suffer loss,
  I go to take thy place,
  To bear thy cross."
Then Peter bowed his head,
Discomfited;
There, at the Master's feet,
Found grace complete,
And courage, and new faith,
And turned—with Him,
To Death.

So we—
Whene'er we fail
Of our full duty,
Cast on Him our load,—
  Who suffered sore for us,
  Who frail flesh wore for us,
  Who all things bore for us—
On Christ, The Lord.

JOHN OXENHAM

SIMON THE CYRENIAN

This is the tale from first to last:—
    Outside Jerusalem
I saw them lead a prisoner past
    With thorns for diadem.
Broken and weak and driven fast
    He fell at my garment's hem.

There stood no other stranger by,
    On me they laid His load.
The Cross whereon He was to die
    I bore along the road,
I saw Him nailed, I heard Him cry
    Forsaken of His God.

Now I am dead as well as He,
    And, marvel strange to tell,
But Him they nailed upon the tree
    Is Lord of Heaven and Hell,
And judgeth who doeth wickedly,
    Rewardeth who doeth well.

He has given to me beacons four,
    A Cross in the southern sky,
In token that His cross I bore
    In His extremity;
For One I never knew before
    The day He came to die.

LUCY LYTTELTON

MEN FOLLOW SIMON

They spat in His face and hewed Him a cross
On that dark day.
The cross was heavy; Simon bore it
Golgotha way.
  O Master, the cross is heavy!

They ripped His hands with driven nails
And flayed Him with whips.
They pressed the sponge of vinegar
To His parched lips.
  O Master, Thy dear blood drips!

Men follow Simon, three and three,
And one and one,
Down through valleys and up long hills
Into the sun.
  O Master, Master—into the sun!

RAYMOND KRESENSKY

SIMON THE CYRENIAN SPEAKS

He never spoke a word to me,
  And yet He called my name,
He never gave a sign to me,
  And yet I knew and came.

At first I said, "I will not bear
  His cross upon my back;
He only seeks to place it there
  Because my skin is black."

But He was dying for a dream,
  And He was very weak,
And in His eyes there shone a gleam
  Men journey far to seek.

It was Himself my pity bought;
  I did for Christ alone
What all of Rome could not have wrought
  With bruise of lash or stone.

COUNTEE CULLEN

THE BLESSED ROAD

Three roads led out to Calvary.
  The first was broad and straight,
That Pilate and great Caiaphas
  Might ride thereon in state.

The second was the felons' road,
  Cruel and hard to tread
For those who bore the cross's load,
  For those whose footsteps bled.

The third road slunk through mean defiles,
  Fearing the open sky;
And Judas crept the dreadful miles
  To Calvary thereby.

The highroad up to Calvary
  Was blotted from the land;
Where Judas hid, the jackal cries
  By thorn-cursed drifts of sand.

But that poor road the felons went—
  How fair it now appears,
Smoothed wide by myriads penitent
  And flower-set by their tears!

CHARLES BUXTON GOING

RECOGNITION

When Christ went up to Calvary,
  His crown upon His head,
Each tree unto its fellow-tree
  In awful silence said:
"Behold the Gardener is He
  Of Eden and Gethsemane!"

JOHN B. TABB

UPON A HILL

Three men shared death upon a hill,
But only one man died;
The other two—
A thief and God Himself—
Made rendezvous.

Three crosses still
Are borne up Calvary's Hill,
Where Sin still lifts them high:
Upon the one, sag broken men
Who, cursing, die;

Another holds the praying thief,
Or those who penitent as he,
Still find the Christ
Beside them on the tree.

Miriam LeFevre Crouse

THE MARTYR

And all the while they mocked Him and reviled,
And heaped upon Him words of infamy,
He stood serenely there, and only smiled
In pity at the blind intensity
Of hate; for well He knew that Love alone
Can cure the ills of men—of nations, too—
Though unregenerate mobs their prophets stone,
And crucify the gentle Christ anew.
So He but smiled, and drained with quiet grace
The bitter cup for lips too eloquent,
And, dauntless, took the soul-degrading place
Designed for thieves—this Prophet heaven-sent!
And when the throng at length had hushed its cry,
Another cross loomed dark against the sky.

Natalie Flohr

GAMBLER

And sitting down, they watched Him there,
The soldiers did;
There, while they played with dice,
He made His sacrifice,

And died upon the cross to rid
God's world of sin.
He was a gambler, too, my Christ,
He took His life and threw
It for a world redeemed.
And ere His agony was done,
Before the westering sun went down,
Crowning that day with crimson crown,
He knew that He had won.

G. A. STUDDERT KENNEDY

THE EARTH WORSHIPED!

A crown of thorns men gave to Christ,
    Who should have worn the bay,
The wreath lay gently on His brow
    And turned its points away.

"If thou be God," men mocking said,
    "Then show to us a sign"—
They did not know the vinegar
    Changed at His lips to wine.

The very earth's foundations shook,
    High heaven veiled its face;
Within a tomb sealed with a stone
    Men made the Lord a place.

The stone rolled outward at His word,
    The linen cloths untwined,
Earth had more reverence than men
    For Him who saved mankind!

CATHERINE CATE COBLENTZ

QUESTION

I wonder if that cypress tree
  Which stood in Eden long ago
And lifted hands where bird and bee
  Winged heaven through the seasons' flow,
Was ever mindful that a day
  Would bring it aching agony,
And it would stand, a cross, to slay
  The Christ of love on Calvary.

HOWARD McKINLEY CORNING

AT JERUSALEM

Jerusalem, Jerusalem, who oft
  His love had gathered thee beneath its wing
And thou wouldst not! Love crucified aloft
  On Calvary, enthroned the King of Kings.

KATHARINE LEE BATES

THE UNIVERSAL GUILT

I saw One greeted with a kiss;
  A son of night performed the deed;
And then they led away my Lord
  To be despised, to suffer, bleed;
And I stood by, nor said a word,
Nor was I by His mute grief stirred.

I saw One wear a crown of thorns;
  They placed it rudely on His brow,
And pressed it down; and as He bowed
  They cried, "Messiah—see Him now!"
And I stood by, nor moved a limb
To save my Lord, or comfort Him.

I saw One hanging on a cross;
  As in each hand they drove the nail,
He groaned and cried, "O God, forgive!"
  They laughed and shouted, "King, all hail!"
And I with them was standing there,
As he breathed out His dying prayer.

THOMAS CURTIS CLARK

GOOD FRIDAY

You drove the nails in His white, white feet;
  I pierced each tender hand:
And we laughed as we lifted the cross on high—
  Too wise to understand.

You gave Him the gall and vinegar;
  I thrust the lance in His side;
Yet they say it was years and years ago
  That the Savior was crucified.

EDGAR DANIEL KRAMER

REVEALMENT

They planned for Christ a cruel death;
  Steel pierced His hands, and feet and side;

They mocked His last expiring breath,
    And thought their hate was satisfied.

They wagged their heads and said, "Lo, He
    Would crush our temple and in three days
Restore its beauty. Come and see
    This boaster gone death's quiet ways."

They did not know that on that hill
    Eternal love was satisfied;
That Christ, who hung there, triumphed still.
    . . . And only cruel death had died!

JOHN RICHARD MORELAND

THE NINTH HOUR

After the shameful trial in the hall,
The mocking and the scourging, and the pain
Of Peter's words; to Herod, and again
To Pilate's judgment-seat, the royal pall,
The cross itself, the vinegar and gall;
The thieves close by, discipleship proved vain,
The scoffing crowd, His mother's tears like rain,
There came one moment, bitterest of all.
Yet in that cry, when flesh and spirit failed,
Last effort of the awful way He trod,
Which shook the earth, nor left the temple veiled,
In that exceeding great and bitter cry
Was conquest. The centurion standing by
Said, Truly this man was the Son of God.

CAROLINE HAZARD

THE MOTHER

There was a trampling of horses from Calvary
   Where the armed Romans rode from the mountain side;
Yet riding they dreamed of the soul that could ride free
   Out of the bruised breast and the arms nailed wide.

There was a trampling of horses from Calvary,
   And the long spears glittered in the night;
Yet riding they dreamed of the will that dared to be,
   When the head fell and the heavens were rent with light.

The eyes that closed over sleep like folded wings
   And the sad mouth that kissed death with the cry
"Father, forgive them,"—silently these things,
   They remembered, riding down from Calvary.

And Joseph, when the sick body was lowered slowly,
   Folded it in a white cloth without seam,
The indomitable brow, inflexible and holy,
   And the sad breast that held the immortal dream.

And the feet that could not walk, and the pierced hand,
   And the arms that held the whole world in their embrace;
But Mary, beside the cross-tree, could not understand,
   Looking upon the tired, human face.

JOHN HALL WHEELOCK

THE CENTURION

A Vision

I saw him leave his pagan century
By stealth, to trail a ruffian mob by night,
And in the circle of a lanthorn's light,
Within the garden called Gethsemane,
Behold in pained bewilderment, the sight
Of Innocence ensnared by treachery . . .
As at a later hour he stood to see
The Sacrifice upon Golgotha's height.

But when he came to call the drunken guard
Sleep-drowned on duty at a vacant tomb,
And saw a thousand lilies gem the sward
Where Jesus walked unfettered in the gloom,
His pale lips smitten by an angel's rod,
Cried out, "I know this is the Son of God!"

HELEN PURCELL ROADS

THE WAY OF THE WORLD

The hands of the king are soft and fair—
    They never knew labor's strain.
The hands of the robber redly wear
    The bloody brand of Cain.
But the hands of the Man are hard and scarred
    With the scars of toil and pain.

The slaves of Pilate have washed their hands
   As white as a king's might be.
Barabbas with wrists unfettered stands,
   For the world has made him free.
But Thy palms toil-worn by nails are torn,
   O Christ, on Calvary.

JAMES JEFFREY ROCHE

THE CRUCIFIXION

   Oh, man's capacity
For spiritual sorrow, corporal pain!
Who has explored the deepmost of that sea,
With heavy links of a far-fathoming chain?

   That melancholy lead,
Let down in guilty and in innocent hold,
Yea into childish hands deliverèd,
Leaves the sequestered floor unreached, untold.

   One only has explored
The deepmost; but He did not die of it.
Not yet, not yet He died. Man's human Lord
Touched the extreme; it is not infinite.

   But over the abyss
Of God's capacity for woe He stayed
One hesitating hour; what gulf was this?
Forsaken He went down, and was afraid!

ALICE MEYNELL

LAST HILL

You who have raised
   And bound me high
Fast to cross
   And think I die,

Tortured by ills,
   The nail and thirst:
Death of the man,
   Despised, accurst:

Little you know
   I died in sweet
Circle of beauty,
   Cool, complete;

Little you know
   I died that night;
Died from a kiss
   By lantern light.

EDITH MIRICK

THE RICH YOUNG MAN

It seemed so mad a thing to do—
To grieve so deep—to perish, too,
For men He never even knew!
A life so lonely, meek and bare!
I wonder why He made a prayer
For them that mocked and nailed Him there!

Vast wealth is mine; why do I see
My golden hoard without avail?
Why turns no man with love to me?
Why did He triumph, and I fail?
Poor and despised! how strange a thing
That mighty hosts, with worshiping,
Their homage to His name should bring!

Oh, 'tis a grievous mystery—
That mankind never looks to me
As to that spent and broken Christ
Who drooped on Calvary!

Laura Simmons

FROM BETHLEHEM TO CALVARY

From Bethlehem to Calvary the Savior's journey lay;
Doubt, unbelief, scorn, fear, and hate beset Him day by day,
But in His heart He bore God's love that brightened all the
way.

O'er the Judean hills He walked, serene and brave of soul,
Seeking the beaten paths of men, touching and making
whole,
Dying at last for love of man, on Calvary's darkened knoll.

He went with patient step and slow, as one who scatters
seed;
Like a fierce hunger in His heart He felt the world's great
need,
And the negations Moses gave He changed to loving deed.

From Bethlehem to Calvary the world still follows on,
Even as the halt and blind of old along His path were
    drawn;
Through Calvary's clouds they seek the light that led Him
    to the dawn.

MEREDITH NICHOLSON

THE WORLD'S LONE LOVER

He was no stranger to salty tears, He
Who died upon a cedar tree;—
He was a brother to ancient grief
And to the trembling olive leaf . . .
Or if you cross the distant bar
He will be friendly as a star,—
As a star, when men at sea,
Have lost the lights along the lee,—
As a star when on some road
One man carries two men's load . . .
He is lover; He is friend;
And compensation at the journey's end . . .
He knows the alchemy of a tear;
He knows why we start and fear;
For He was flesh and knew why pain
Ceased for a day and came again;
He felt the flesh's blow and smart,
Caught life's arrow in His heart,
But smiled—smiled and then forgave—
There is no darkness in His grave.

J. R. PERKINS

CONTRAST

And it was in the winter
   When all the world was bare
That God came down to Bethlehem
   And found a shelter there.

But it was in the springtime
   When all was bright and fair
They took our God to Calvary
   And let Him suffer there.

CHARLES GRENVILLE HAMILTON

THE CROSS WAS HIS OWN

They borrowed a bed to lay His head
   When Christ the Lord came down;
They borrowed the ass in the mountain pass
   For Him to ride to town;
But the crown that He wore and the Cross that He bore
   Were His own—
     The Cross was His own.

He borrowed the bread when the crowd He fed
   On the grassy mountain side,
He borrowed the dish of broken fish
   With which He satisfied.
But the crown that He wore and the Cross that He bore
   Were His own—
     The Cross was His own.

He borrowed the ship in which to sit
  To teach the multitude;
He borrowed a nest in which to rest—
  He had never a home so rude;
But the crown that He wore and the Cross that He bore
  Were His own—
  The Cross was His own.

He borrowed a room on His way to the tomb
  The Passover Lamb to eat;
They borrowed a cave for Him a grave,
They borrowed a winding sheet.
But the crown that He wore and the Cross that He bore
  Were His own—
  The Cross was His own.

AUTHOR UNKNOWN

I AM THE CROSS

I am the Cross of Christ!
I bore His body there
  On Calvary's lonely hill.
Till then I was a humble tree
  That grew beside a tiny rill;
I think till then
I was a thing despised of men!

I am the Cross of Christ!
I grew, and sapped the water
  From that little stream;
I loved the sun and heard the winds
  And dreamed my humble dream.
And thus it was until
They took me to that pain-hurt hill.

I am the Cross of Christ!
I felt His limbs along
  My common, broken bark;
I saw His utter loneliness,
  The lightning and the dark;
And up till then
I thought He was as other men.

I am the Cross of Christ!
I crown the pointed spires
  Of man-made temples near and far.
I watch the rising and the setting
  Of each far-flung star;
All through the night I am
Eternal Sentinel for Man!

I am the Cross of Christ!
My form they used to crucify
  The outcasts of the earth;
But on that lonely hill that day
  My kind received, in blood, new birth,
And ever till this day
A weary world bows at my feet to pray!

I am the Cross of Christ!
They say I tower "o'er the wrecks
Of time." I only know
That once, a humble tree,
This was not so. But this
I know—since then
I have become a symbol for the hopes of men.

WILLIAM L. STIDGER

LOVE'S WAY

I never realized God's birth before,
How He grew likest God in being born.
Such ever was love's way—to rise, it stoops.

From The Ring and the Book   ROBERT BROWNING

THE SOVEREIGN EMBLEM

Whatso'er
The form of building or the creed professed,
The Cross, bold type of shame to homage turned,
Of an unfinished life that sways the world,
Shall tower as sovereign emblem over all.

From The Cathedral   JAMES RUSSELL LOWELL

WAKING THOUGHT

Waking I look to Jesus on the Rood
　And thank Him that the ghostly night is gone;
Until my soul had seen the Holy Cross
　I never knew the dawn.

All colors were as darkness save the hues
　That even our dull bodily eyes can see,
But now is God grown fair beyond the East
　Upon His blessed tree.

MARGUERITE WILKINSON

THERE IS A MAN ON THE CROSS

Whenever there is silence around me
By day or by night—
I am startled by a cry.
It came down from the cross—
The first time I heard it.
I went out and searched—
And found a Man in the throes of crucifixion,
And I said, "I will take You down,"
And I tried to take the nails out of His feet.
But He said, "Let them be
For I cannot be taken down
Until every man, every woman, and every child
Come together to take Me down."
And I said, "But I cannot hear You cry.
What can I do?"
And he said, "Go about the world—
Tell everyone that you meet—
There is a Man on the cross."

ELIZABETH CHENEY

MY MASTER

My Master was so very poor,
A manger was His cradling place;
So very rich my Master was
Kings came from far
To gain His grace.

My Master was so very poor
And with the poor He broke the bread;
So very rich my Master was
That multitudes
By Him were fed.

My Master was so very poor
They nailed Him naked to a cross;
So very rich my Master was
He gave His all
And knew no loss.

HARRY LEE

THE PASSION FLOWER

Thou lowly, meek and lovely flower,
But yesterday, at evening's hour,
As trudged I upward with my load,
I saw thee blooming by the road,
And stayed my steps to wonder there
That beauty so supremely fair
Should waste its loveliness on me—
Even as the Flower of Calvary!

CHARLES G. BLANDEN

MEDITATION IN ST. MARY'S

Do gold-tongued candles comfort Thee
Who tasted darkness on a tree?
Can altar lilies drain
Thy side of pain?

Does perfumed prayer
Thy hands repair,
Or swiftly taken bread
Ease Thy thorned head, Jesu?

GERTRUDE DU BOIS

HIS HANDS

The hands of Christ
Seem very frail,
For they were broken
By a nail.

But only they reach
Heaven at last
Whom these frail, broken
Hands hold fast.

JOHN RICHARD MORELAND

VIA CRUCIS

Out of the dark we come, nor know
Into what outer dark we go.
Wings sweep across the stars at night,
Sweep and are lost in flight,
And down the star-strewn windy lanes the sky
Is empty as before the wings went by.
We dare not lift our eyes, lest we should see
The utter quiet of eternity;
So, in the end, we come to this:
Christ-Mary's kiss.

We cannot brook the wide sun's might,
We are alone and chilled by night;
We stand, atremble and afraid,
Upon the small worlds we have made;
Fearful, lest all our poor control
Should turn and tear us to the soul;
A dread, lest we should be denied
The price we hold our ragged pride;
So in the end we cast them by
For a gaunt cross against the sky.

To those who question is the fine reward
Of the brave heart who fights with broken sword
In the dark night against an unseen enemy;
There is not any hope of victory.
While sweat is sweet and earthly ways and toil,
The touch of shoulders, scent of new-turned soil,
Striving itself amid the thrusting throng,
And love that comes with white hands strong;
But on itself the long path turns again,
To find at length the hill of pain.

Such only do we know and see;
Starlight and evening mystery,
Sunlight on peaks and dust-red plain,
Thunder and the quick breath of rain,
Stirring of fields and all the lovely things
That season after season brings;
Young dawn and quiet night
And the earth's might.
But all our wisdom and our wisdom's plan
End in the lonely figure of a Man.

MAXWELL STRUTHERS BURT

A MAN AND GOD

They walked and talked—a Man and God;
A fragrance lingered where they trod,
A music circled as they spoke,
And over them a glory broke.

They talked and walked, down many years—
The way was called The Vale of Tears;
But He who walked with God received
Such comfort that He little grieved.

And walking thus, and talking so,
The Man and God fared onward slow,
Until they reached a secret spot—
God took Him, and the Man was not.

JOHN T. MCFARLAND

III

EASTER DAY BREAKS!

EASTER DAY BREAKS!

Easter day breaks!
Christ rises! Mercy every way is infinite—
Earth breaks up; time drops away;
In flows heaven with its new day
Of endless life—
What is left for us save in growth
Of soul to rise up . . .
From the gift looking to the giver,
And from the cistern to the river,
And from the finite to infinity,
And from man's dust to God's divinity.

ROBERT BROWNING

EASTER NIGHT

All night had shout of men and cry
   Of woeful women filled His way;
Until that noon of somber sky
   On Friday, clamor and display
Smote Him; no solitude had He,
No silence, since Gethsemane.

Public was Death; but Power, but Might,
   But Life again, but Victory,

Were hushed within the dead of night,
  The shuttered dark, the secrecy.
And all alone, alone, alone
He rose again behind the stone.

ALICE MEYNELL

A GUARD OF THE SEPULCHER

I was a Roman soldier in my prime;
Now age is on me and the yoke of time.
I saw your Risen Christ, for I am he
Who reached the hyssop to Him on the tree;
And I am one of two who watched beside
The Sepulcher of Him we crucified.

All that last night I watched with sleepless eyes;
Great stars arose and crept across the skies.
The world was all too still for mortal rest,
For pitiless thoughts were busy in the breast.
The night was long, so long, it seemed at last
I had grown old and a long life had passed.
Far off, the hills of Moab, touched with light,
Were swimming in the hollow of the night.
I saw Jerusalem all wrapped in cloud,
Stretched like a dead thing folded in a shroud.

Once in the pauses of our whispered talk,
I heard a something on the garden walk.
Perhaps it was a crisp leaf lightly stirred—
Perhaps the dream-note of a waking bird.

Then suddenly an angel burning white
Came down with earthquake in the breaking light,
And rolled the great stone from the Sepulcher,
Mixing the morning with a scent of myrrh.
And lo, the Dead had risen with the day:
The Man of Mystery had gone His way!

Years have I wandered, carrying my shame;
Now let the tooth of time eat out my name.
For we, who all the wonder might have told,
Kept silence, for our mouths were stopt with gold.

EDWIN MARKHAM

THE SEPULCHER IN THE GARDEN

What though the Flowers in Joseph's Garden grew
Of rarest perfume and of fairest hue,
That morn when Magdalene hastened through
    Its fragrant, silent paths?

She caught no scent of budding almond tree;
Her eyes, tear-blinded still from Calvary,
Saw neither lily nor anemone—
    Naught save the Sepulcher.

But when the Master whispered "Mary," lo!
The Tomb was hid; the Garden all aglow;
And burst in bloom the Rose of Jericho—
    From that day "Mary's Flower."

JOHN FINLEY

MARY

On the first Easter, ere the harbinger
Of that new Dawn its first low note had sung,
While o'er the garden grieving night yet hung
And Mary waited by the sepulcher,
I wonder if the silence held for her
The echo of a courtly Eastern tongue;
If, bearing spikenard, she yet bravely clung
To memory of frankincense and myrrh.
Still did she keep the glory of Bethlehem,
Pondering the marvels at the manger's side,
So in her hour of darkness comforted?
Or did the cross outside Jerusalem,
Where with dimmed eyes she saw Him crucified,
Shadow all else but this: "My Son is dead"?

NELLIE KNIGHT

MARY MAGDALENE

At dawn she sought the Savior slain,
To kiss the spot where He had lain
And weep warm tears, like springtime rain;

When lo, there stood, unstained of death,
A man that spoke with low sweet breath;
And "Master!" Mary answereth.

From out the far and fragrant years
How sweeter than the songs of seers
That tender offering of tears!

RICHARD BURTON

ACCORDING TO ST. MARK

The way was steep and wild; we watched Him go
Through tangled thicket, over sharp-edged stone
That tore His feet, until He stood alone
Upon the summit where four great winds blow;
Fearful we knelt on the cold rocks below,
For the o'erhanging cloud had larger grown,
A strange still radiance through His Body shone
Whiter than moonlight on the mountain snow.

Then two that flamed amber and amethyst
Were either side Him, while low thunder rolled
Down to the ravens in their dark ravine;
But when we looked again, as through a mist
We saw Him near us.—Like a pearl we hold
Close to our hearts what we have heard and seen.

THOMAS S. JONES, JR.

THE ALL-LOVING

So, the All-Great were the All-Loving too—
So, through the thunder comes a human voice
Saying, "O heart I made, a heart beats here!
Face, my hands fashioned, see it in myself.
Thou hast no power nor may'st conceive of mine,
But love I gave thee, with myself to love,
And thou must love me who have died for thee!"

ROBERT BROWNING

From CHRISTMAS EVE

Earth breaks up, time drops away,
In flows heaven, with its new day
Of endless life, when He who trod,
Very Man and Very God,
This Earth in weakness, shame and pain,
Dying the death whose signs remain
Up yonder on the accursed tree—
Shall come again, no more to be
Of Captivity the thrall,
But the One God, all in all,
King of Kings and Lord of Lords,
As His servant John received the words,
"I died, and live forevermore!"

ROBERT BROWNING

TOMBS

Egyptian tombs hold priceless things,
Sceptres and crowns and rings,
And ornaments of cunning skill
To humor the imperial will
Of mummied potentates.
Full tombs,
Great corridors and rooms,
To tell of ancient powers and high estates.

And has an empty tomb no glory shed?
"He is not here; He is risen," angels said.

LOUISE WEBSTER

EASTER JOY

I, too, O Christ, denied you,
  And felt the dawn-winds blow
Cold and gray upon my cheek,
  And heard the cock's loud crow;

I, too, sat silent while the scribes
  With cynic wisdom tried,
Buffeted, reviled and mocked,
  Condemned you—crucified.

But I have seen the dead arise,
  The spring wake fair and strong;
And doubt has changed to soaring faith,
  Despair to love and song.

DAISY CONWAY PRICE

CHRIST IS ARISEN

Christ is arisen,
  Joy to thee, mortal!
Out of His prison,
  Forth from its portal!
Christ is not sleeping,
  Seek Him no longer;
Strong was His keeping,
  Jesus was stronger.

Christ is arisen,
  Seek Him not here;
Lonely His prison,
  Empty His bier;

Vain His entombing,
   Spices and lawn,
Vain the perfuming,
   Jesus is gone.

Christ is arisen,
   Joy to thee, mortal!
Empty His prison,
   Broken its portal!
Rising, He giveth
   His shroud to the sod;
Risen, He liveth,
   And liveth to God.

From Easter Hymn in Faust   J. W. VON GOETHE

RESURRECTION

In this brown seed, so dry and hard,
I see a flower in my door yard.
You, chrysalis in winding sheet,
Are butterfly all dainty sweet.
All life is warmed by spring's sweet breath,
And Christ our Lord has conquered death.

AGNES W. STORER

AN OLIVE TREE SPEAKS

That night in cool Gethsemane
Christ taught us immortality.
We heard Him pray beneath our boughs
And felt His wrestling spirit's vows

While high upon her ancient hills,
Jerusalem, walled in smugness, slept
Nor guessed that her own Savior wept
Beyond the Kedron's full spring rills.

We trembled with His lonely woes,
We longed to crash on all His foes,
We saw His face when He arose—a Conqueror!

So for His sake we cannot die,
But from our gnarled, decrepit root
Send up a new young slender shoot
To tell His victory to the sky.
Before our old self bows to earth,
We give a scion olive birth
To witness what we learned that night
When Christ slew death within our sight
And to our hushed Gethsemane
Entrusted immortality.

MADELEINE SWEENY MILLER

EASTER MUSIC

Blow, golden trumpets, sweet and clear,
Blow soft upon the perfumed air;
Bid the sad earth to join our song,
"To Christ does victory belong!"

Oh, let the winds your message bear
To every heart of grief and care;
Sound through the world the joyful lay,
"Our Christ hath conquered Death today!"

On cloudy wings let glad words fly
Through the soft blue of echoing sky:
Ring out, O trumpets, sweet and clear,
"Through Death immortal Life is here!"

MARGARET WADE DELAND

HOPE

He died!

And with Him perished all that men hold dear;
Hope lay beside Him in the sepulcher,
Love grew corse cold, and all things beautiful beside
　　　　Died when He died.

He rose!

And with Him hope arose, and life and light.
Men said, "Not Christ but Death died yesternight."
And joy and truth and all things virtuous
　　　　Rose when He rose.

AUTHOR UNKNOWN

CHRIST HAS RISEN

Christ has risen—else in vain
All the sunshine, all the rain,
All the warmth and quickening,
And renewal of the spring.
Vain they were to charm our eyes,
Greening earth and gracious skies,

Growth and beauty, bud or bloom,
If within their fast-sealed tomb
All our dearer dead must dwell,
Sharing not the miracle.

Crocus tips in shining row,
Welcome, for your sign we know.
Every bud on every bough
Has its message for us now,
Since the Lord on Easter Day
Burst the bonds of prisoning clay;
All the springtime has a voice,
Every heart may dare rejoice,
Every grave, no more a prison.
Joins the chorus, "Christ is risen."

SUSAN COOLIDGE

RESURRECTION

Ye who fear death,
Behold the buds are bursting;
Ye who fear death,
Hark, how the robins sing;
Ye who fear death,
Go hear the crocus crying,
Eternal Spring!

Ye who fear death,
See how the trees are greening,
Risen to life before the April sun;
Ye who fear death,
Give way to joy and gladness,
New life's begun!

So has it been
Since days first had beginning,
Glad prophecies of Resurrection Morn;
Weep not before a closed tomb
In Joseph's garden,
Life is reborn!

RALPH S. CUSHMAN

RESURGAM

It happened on an April day,
    Bounded by skies so blue and still,
And olive trees all hushed and gray,
    They led One up a skull-shaped hill
Followed by a crowd whose piercing cry
Was, "Crucify!"

It happened on an April morn,
    They nailed a Man upon a tree
Whose head was circled with sharp thorn,
    Lifted Him high that all might see
His agony, His heaving breath,
His awful death.

It happened on an April eve—
    The air was cut by one sharp cry
That wine nor gall could not relieve:
    "Eli . . . lama . . . Sabachthani' . . .
Then lightning, thunder crack on crack,
The sun was black.

It happened on an April day . . .
    They tombed a Man (the crowd had fled)

Sealed it; and set a watch that way
    To flout His words; to prove Him dead;
And show Himself He could not save
From the dark grave.

It happened on an April day . . .
    A tremor shook the paling gloom,
A white flame tore the door away,
    Life came a victor from the tomb.
Love cannot die, nor truth betray . . .
Christ rose upon an April day!

JOHN RICHARD MORELAND

EASTER

Lord, now that Spring is in the world,
    And every tulip is a cup
Filled with the wine of Thy great love,
    Lift Thou me up.

Raise Thou my heart as flowers arise
    To greet the glory of Thy day,
With soul as clean as lilies are,
    And white as they.

Let me not fear the darkness now,
    Since Life and Light break through Thy tomb;
Teach me that doubts no more oppress,
    No more consume.

Show me that Thou art April, Lord,
    And Thou the flowers and the grass;

Then, when awake the soft Spring winds,
　I'll hear Thee pass!

CHARLES HANSON TOWNE

RESURRECTION AND ASCENSION

He built a kingdom with His heart and brain,
He knew hosannas and the psalms, till one
Played Judas for a paltry little gain,
And in that hour His kingdom was undone.
His spirit entering Gethsemane,
Enduring bitter, bitter hours alone,
At last went staggering to Calvary,
From thence to hell—and found a bed of stone.

But when the lilies flamed He breathed again,
A man of scars, yet luminous and strange
With ecstasy unknown to other men—
An ecstasy no Judas kiss may change.
The hosts who fled now worship from afar:
They kneel before the beauty of a star.

EARL D. TODD

THE ASCENSION

The Testimony of Mary Magdalene

In the gray dawn they left Jerusalem,
And I rose up to follow after them.
He led toward Bethany by the narrow bridge
Of Kedron, upward to the olive ridge.

Once on the camel path beyond the City,
He looked back, struck at heart with pain and pity—
Looked backward from the two lone cedar trees
On Olivet, alive to every breeze—
Looked in a rush of sudden tears, and then
Went steadily on, never to turn again.

Near the green quiets of a little wood
The Master halted silently and stood.
The figs were purpling, and a fledgling dove
Had fallen from a windy bough above,
And lay there crying feebly by a thorn,
Its little body bruisèd and forlorn.
He stept aside a moment from the rest
And put it safely back into the nest.

Then mighty words did seem to rise in Him
And die away; even as white vapors swim
A moment on Mount Carmel's purple steep,
And then are blown back rainless to the deep.
And once He looked up with a little start:
Perhaps some loved name passed across his heart,
Some memory of a road in Galilee,
Or old familiar rock beside the Sea.

And suddenly there broke upon our sight
A rush of angels terrible with light—
The high same host the Shepherds saw go by,
Breaking the starry night with lyric cry—
A rush of angels, wistful and aware,
That shook a thousand colors on the air—
Colors that made a music to the eye—

Glories of lilac, azure, gold, vermilion,
Blown from the air-hung delicate pavilion.
And now His face grew bright with luminous will:
The great grave eyes grew planet-like and still.
Yea, in that moment, all His face, fire-white,
Seemed struck out of imperishable light.
Delicious apprehension shook His spirit,
With song so still that only the heart could hear it.
A sense of something sacred, starry, vast,
Greater than earth, across the watchers passed.

Then with a stretching of His hands to bless,
A last unspeakable look that was caress,
Up through the vortice of bright cherubim
He rose until the august form grew dim—
Up through the blue dome of the day ascended,
By circling flights of seraphim befriended.
He was uplifted from us, and was gone
Into the darkness of another dawn.

EDWIN MARKHAM

IV

THE CONTINUING CHRIST

THE CONTINUING CHRIST

Far, far away is Bethlehem,
  And years are long and dim
Since Mary held the holy Child
  And angels sang to Him:
But still to hearts where love and faith
  Make room for Christ in them,
He comes again, the Child from God,
  To find His Bethlehem.

Beyond the sea is Galilee,
  And ways which Jesus trod,
And hidden there are those high hills
  Where He communed with God;
Yet on the plains of common life
  Through all the world of men,
The voice that once said, "Follow me,"
  Speaks to our hearts again.

Gethsemane and Calvary,
  And death and bitter loss,
Are these but echoes drifting down
  From a forgotten cross?
Nay, Lord, for all our living sins
  Thy cross is lifted up,
And as of old we hear Thee say,
  "Can ye too drink My cup?"

O Life that seems so long ago,
　And yet is ever new,
The fellowship of love with Thee,
　Through all the years is true.
O Master over death and time,
　Reveal Thyself, we pray,
And as before amongst Thine own,
　So dwell with us today!

W. Russell Bowie

I KNOW A ROAD

I know a road in Palestine—
　A long, strange, winding way
That runs and rises to the hills,
　Then slips down to the bay;

The road starts out at Bethlehem,
　On Judah's fertile plain,
And passes by a manger bare,
　In which a babe has lain.

It winds where Jordan's fertile bank
　Turns to a stony crest,
And far into the wilderness,
　Where One has stood the test.

It twists and twines up hill and down,
　By postern-gate and wall,
Through country, village, city, town,
　Past palace, hut and stall.

It lingers by still Galilee,
   As if to rest awhile;
Then hastens to the hills again,
   In one long, curving smile.

It listens here, as if to words
   Its friends, the trees, would say,
As, bending o'er it lovingly,
   They lift their arms to pray.

It hesitates, as if to ask,
   If it should still go on,
Then lifts its head to do its task,
   And runs on straight and strong.

It broadens out before the gate,
   Rests near the olive tree,
Then leads into Jerusalem,
   Where all the world may see.

Then past the temple pillars tall
   It winds in majesty;
It seems to have no end at all—
   On, up past Calvary.

And on and on, down through the years—
   On goes this way of ways;
It levels out the mountain's fears
   And sings the valley's praise.

It does not end in Palestine;
   It runs the world around;
You need not seek the holy land
   To see its beauty crowned.

It is as rough-hewn, and as hard,
　　Today as e'er before;
You too may see the bleeding feet
　　As they go by your door.

It is a sun-baked, stony road,
　　But some who walk it find
The footprints of a Traveler,
　　With love upon His mind;

With sunshine in the face of Him,
　　With joy in word and way,
And strength to share your load if you
　　Will walk with Him today.

　　　　　　　　　　CARL VINTON HERRON

REALITY

Not from two who supped with You
　　At an inn as twilight fell
Do I know that Joseph's tomb
　　Was an empty shell.

Not from Peter or from John
　　Or from Mary or from Paul
Did I learn how life can change
　　At Your call.

Not on the Damascus road
　　Or in any far off place
Did my spirit see the dawn
　　Of Your face.

Those who lived in Galilee
Knew their Lord and held Him dear—
But my Lord has come to me
Now and here.

AMELIA JOSEPHINE BURR

IT IS NOT FINISHED, LORD

It is not finished, Lord.
There is not one thing done.
There is no battle of my life
That I have really won.
And now I come to tell Thee
How I fought to fail.
I cannot read this writing of the years;
My eyes are full of tears.
It gets all blurr'd and won't make sense.
It's full of contradictions
Like the scribblings of a child.
I can but hand it in, and hope
That Thy great mind, which reads
The writings of so many lives,
Will understand this scrawl
And what it strives
To say—but leaves unsaid.
I cannot write it over.
The stars are coming out.
My body needs its bed.
I have no strength for more,
So it must stand or fall—dear Lord!—
That's all.

G. A. STUDDERT KENNEDY

I HAVE OVERCOME THE WORLD

Thy crown of empire—must thou yield it now?
(Mine was of thorns they pressed upon My brow;)

Did friends, as foes, desert thee in thy power?
(Mine could not watch with Me one single hour.)

Is all thy life stripped stark through shame and loss?
(Between two thieves I hung—upon a Cross.)

LAURA SIMMONS

AND CHRIST IS CRUCIFIED ANEW

Not only once, and long ago,
There on Golgotha's rugged side,
Has Christ, the Lord, been crucified
Because He loved a lost world so.
But hourly souls, sin-satisfied,
Mock His great love, flout His commands.
And I drive nails deep in His hands,
You thrust the spear within His side.

JOHN RICHARD MORELAND

NOT YOURS BUT YOU

He died for me: what can I offer Him?
Towards Him swells incense of perpetual prayer;
His court wear crowns and aureoles round their hair:
His ministers are subtle Cherubim;

Ring within ring, white intense Seraphim
Leap like immortal lightnings through the air.
What shall I offer Him? Defiled and bare
My spirit broken and my brightness dim?
"Give Me thy youth." "I yield it to Thy rod,
As Thou didst yield Thy prime of youth for me."
"Give Me thy life." "I give it breath by breath;
As Thou didst give Thy life so give I Thee."
"Give Me thy love." "So be it, my God, my God
As Thou hast loved me, even to bitter death."

CHRISTINA ROSSETTI

THE POTION

Life's burnished grail I take from Him—
A chalice I must drain from brim
Clear down to acid, dreggy stem;

Shall I complain if it be filled
With gall, or brine from tears distilled?
Nay, Lord, I'll drink what Thou hast willed.

But, God, of Thy love give me this sign:
Sometimes let laughter, fragrant, fine,
Make of the draught a bubbling wine.

WINNIE LYNCH ROCKETT

SYMBOLS

I never see upon a hill
    Cedar, or pine or olive tree,

But that I think of One who died
     On Calvary.

I never hear the hammer's ring
     Driving the nail deep in the wood,
But that I see pale hands whose palms
     Are red with blood.

I never feel the dark come down
     But that I hear a piercing cry
That tears my heart.   "Eli . . . Lama . . .
     Sabachthani!"

                              JOHN RICHARD MORELAND

DERELICTION

"Eloi, eloi, lama sabacthani"

I have seen morning break within His eyes
     That caught the heavenly light;
And I have seen in Him the midnight skies
     The very night of night.

I have seen God within that morning glow;
     But not before His cry,
My God, why hast Thou left me? did I know
     That God could be so nigh.

The shrine was brightest with the lamp withdrawn;
     His winter was my spring;
His midnight cry the voices of my dawn;
     The Crucified, my King!

                              EDWARD SHILLITO

WITH ME IN PARADISE

If I had sat at supper with the Lord
And laid my head upon that saving breast
I might have turned and fled among the rest—
I might have been that one who left the board
To add the high priest's silver to his hoard.
Had our Redeemer stooped to wash my feet,
Would I have washed my neighbor's, clean and sweet,
Or thrice denied the Christ I had adored?

Long have I grieved that I was not Saint Paul
Who rode those seas and saw the tempest toss
The ships he sailed in when he heard the call
To preach the risen Christ and gain through loss.

Tonight I envy most among them all
That thief who hung repentant on his cross.

ALEXANDER HARVEY

WHAT IS IT JESUS SAITH?

What is it Jesus saith unto the soul?
"Take up the cross, and come and follow Me."
One word He saith to all men: none may be
Without a cross yet hope to touch the goal.
Then heave it bravely up, and brace thy whole
Body to bear: it will not weigh on thee
Past strength; or if it crush thee to thy knee
Take heart of grace, for grace shall be thy dole.

Give thanks today, and let tomorrow take
Heed to itself; today imports thee more.
Tomorrow may not dawn like yesterday:
Until that unknown morrow go thy way,
Suffer and work and strive for Jesus' sake—
Who tells thee what tomorrow keeps in store?

CHRISTINA ROSSETTI

THE CUP

If now unto my lips be raised,
  The brimming cup of bitter gall,
Grant Thy great strength, dear Lord, and I
  Will drink it all.

My lips may quiver, and my faint heart quail,
  And I may cry at its dread call;
Hold Thou my hand, dear Lord, and I
  .Will drink it all.

FREDERICK T. ROBERTS

LITANY

Oh, by Thy cross and passion, by Thy pain,
Thy resurrection and eternal reign,
From blindness of the soul whose certain doom
Is death, ere yet we moulder in the tomb,
  Deliver us!

From love that cannot see beyond the grave,
However tender, or however brave,
But would—as if this pilgrimage were all—
The ointment bring, the winding-sheet, the pall,
  Deliver us!

Remember not, we pray, our foolish ways,
The fear, the doubt that move us still to raise
Walls around Thee who loved the hungry crowds—
But shame us with Thine own discarded shrouds,
    O Lamb of God!

Life, Life and ever more abundant Life!
Bread of Thy flesh to man us in the strife,
Wine of Thy blood and fervor of Thy flame
Give us to dream, dare, triumph in Thy Name,
    O Lamb of God!

MARIE LeNART

A LENTEN PRAYER

Dear Lord, who sought at dawn of day
The solitary woods to pray;
In quietness we come to ask
Thy guidance for the daily task.

O Master, who with kindly face
At noonday trod the market place,
We crave a brother's smile and song
While mingling in the lonely throng.

Strong Pilot, who at midnight hour,
Could calm the sea with gentle power;
Grant us the skill to aid the bark
Of those who drift in storm and dark.

HARRY WEBB FARRINGTON

THE KING PASSES

The King has passed along the great highway
Where throngs of eager, curious crowds proclaim His praise;
I was so far away—indifferently I gazed,
When, lo! He spoke so clear
I heard as though quite near,
"Come unto Me all ye who labor, and I will give you rest."

(And I who labored not, longed to be blest.)
My heart awoke—my hands reached out and up.
I labor now, unceasingly,
To fill life's empty cup,
That He may stoop and give at last
The blessing promised, as He passed.

ANNE HUNTER TEMPLE

THE VOICE OF CHRISTMAS

I cannot put the Presence by, of Him, the Crucified,
Who moves men's spirits with His love as doth the moon
the tide;
Again I see the Life He lived, the godlike Death He died.

Again I see upon the cross that great Soul-battle fought,
Into the texture of the world the tale of which is wrought
Until it hath become the woof of human deed and thought—

And, joining with the cadenced bells that all the morning
fill,

His cry of agony doth yet my inmost being thrill,
Like some fresh grief from yesterday that tears the heart-
strings still.

I cannot put His presence by, I meet Him everywhere;
I meet Him in the country town, the busy market-square;
The Mansion and the Tenement attest His presence there.

Upon the funneled ships at sea He sets His shining feet;
The Distant Ends of Empire not in vain His Name re-
peat,—
And, like the presence of a rose, He makes the whole world
sweet.

He comes to break the barriers down raised up by barren
creeds;
About the globe from zone to zone, like sunlight He pro-
ceeds;
He comes to give the World's starved heart the perfect love
it needs—

The Christ whose friends have played Him false, whom
Dogmas have belied,
Still speaking to the hearts of men—though shamed and
crucified,
The Master of the centuries who will not be denied!

HARRY KEMP

JESUS OF NAZARETH PASSES BY

Unshaken by the storms that rage
O'er all the earth, in every time,

Moves one lone Man through every age,
  Serene, invincible, sublime.
Through all the centuries He goes,
  His timeless journey to complete
Divinely calm, as one who knows
  The way is sure beneath His feet.

Wild storms of hate beat round His head,
  Earth rocks beneath the crash of war,
But still, with smooth, unhurried tread,
  He moves, untroubled as before.
Over the wrecks of fallen states,
  Through fair, proud nations yet to fall,
Passes the Master of their fates,
  The silent Sovereign of them all.

Unfaltering through the darkest night,
  Denied by man, though loving man,
His face gives back the morning light,
  His calm eyes see God's finished plan.
One little troubled day we bide,
  And then find rest in beds of clay;
But our brief day is glorified—
  We have seen Jesus pass this way.

GEORGE T. LIDDELL

THE SPLENDID LOVER

One and one only is the splendid Lover,
  The all-forgiving, all-compassionate;
When others fret you with impatient loving,
  He a greater Lover patiently will wait.

Though you turn from Him three-score times and seven,
　Mock His devotion, spurn Him as a guest,
With steadfast wooing, He at last will win you,
　And reveal life's wonder when your head lies on His
　　breast.

JOHN RICHARD MORELAND

HE—THEY—WE

They hailed Him King as He passed by,
　They strewed their garments in the road,
But they were set on earthly things,
　And He on God.

They sang His praise for that He did,
　But gave His message little thought;
They could not see that their souls' good
　Was all He sought.

They could not understand why He,
　With powers so vast at His command,
Should hesitate to claim their rights
　And free the land.

Their own concerns and this world's hopes
　Shut out the wonder of His news;
And we, with larger knowledge, still
　His Way refuse.

He walks among us still, unseen,
　And still points out the only way,
But we still follow other gods
　And Him betray.

JOHN OXENHAM

CITIZEN OF THE WORLD

No longer of Him be it said,
"He hath no place to lay His head."

In every land a constant lamp
Flames by His small and mighty camp.

There is no strange and distant place
That is not gladdened by His face.

And every nation kneels to hail
The Splendor shining through its veil.

Cloistered beside the shouting street,
Silent, He calls me to His feet.

Imprisoned for His love of me
He makes my spirit greatly free.

And through my lips that uttered sin
The King of Glory enters in.

JOYCE KILMER

PRAESTO

Expecting Him, my door was open wide:
Then I looked round
If any lack of service might be found,
And saw Him at my side:
How entered, by what secret stair,
I know not, knowing only He was there.

THOMAS EDWARD BROWN

THE LIVING TITHE

Ten met the Master in a field,
Called to Him, agonized, were healed.
Nine hastened on their various ways.
One only, cleansed, returned to praise
Lettered in gratitude and grace,
Meeting his Master face to face.

Let me give thanks! O number me
Among that lesser company.

MABEL MUNNS CHARLES

COMRADE JESUS

I tramped the pavements, cursing God,
When there beside me Jesus trod!

Now we shall walk, my Friend and I,
Across the earth, the sea, the sky.

I do not know what He may be;
I only know He walks with me.

From Eden barred and Paradise,
Too wisely sad, too sadly wise!

Oh, lonely feet! Oh, bleeding feet!
In step with mine on the city street!

RALPH CHEYNEY

AS HE WALKED WITH US

Calm, strong and gentle Man of Galilee,
Whose heart by every human voice is stirred;
By whom are plaintive cries of creatures heard;
Whose eye escapes no tracery of tree,
Or modest wayside flower; alert to see
The fantasy of cloud, the flight of bird;
Whose ear can catch the faintest note and word
Of wind and stream, and distant western sea;
When I am treading on the open space,
Or threading slowly through the crowded marts,
Skilled Craftsman of the woods and market-place,
Companion to all life and human hearts,
I crave, Thou unseen, understanding Guide,
To find Thee, silent, walking by my side.

HARRY WEBB FARRINGTON

NOT ALL THE CROSSES

Not all the crosses are on hills
  Against a livid sky,
Not all the riven hands are scarred,
  Nor all the pierced hearts die!

We face a thousand little deaths
  That none may see or guess
What searing wounds we hide beneath
  Our body's loveliness.

The little song that missed its way,
  Love, patient and unclaimed,
Old scornful words whose memory
  Still turns us sick and shamed,—

A smile that flicked a scorpion lash,
  Grey eyes that did not heed,
The friend beloved and leaned upon
  Who failed us in our need!

Not all the crosses are on hills,—
  And oh, God, keep in sight
Those who come down from Calvary
  With hands unscarred and white!

LUCILE KENDRICK

JESUS OF THE SCARS

If we never sought, we seek Thee now;
  Thine eyes burn through the dark, our only stars;
We must have sight of thorn-pricks on Thy brow,
  We must have Thee, O Jesus of the Scars.

The heavens frighten us; they are too calm;
  In all the universe we have no place.
Our wounds are hurting us; where is the balm?
  Lord Jesus, by Thy Scars we claim Thy grace.

If when the doors are shut, Thou drawest near,
  Only reveal those hands, that side of Thine;
We know today what wounds are, have no fear,
  Show us Thy Scars, we know the countersign.

The other gods were strong; but Thou wast weak;
  They rode, but Thou didst stumble to a throne;
But to our wounds God's wounds alone can speak,
  And not a god has wounds, but Thou alone.

                                        EDWARD SHILLITO

A LITTLE PARABLE

I made the cross myself whose weight
    Was later laid on me.
This thought is torture as I toil
    Up life's steep Calvary.

To think mine own hands drove the nails!
    I sang a merry song,
And chose the heaviest wood I had
    To build it firm and strong.

If I had guessed—if I had dreamed
    Its weight was meant for me,
I should have made a lighter cross
    To bear up Calvary!

                                    ANNE REEVE ALDRICH

A VIRILE CHRIST

Give us a virile Christ for these rough days!
You painters, sculptors, show the warrior bold;
And you who turn mere words to gleaming gold,
Too long your lips have sounded in the praise

Of patience and humility. Our ways
Have parted from the quietude of old;
We need a man of strength with us to hold
The very breach of Death without amaze.
Did He not scourge from temple courts the thieves?
And make the arch-fiend's self again to fall?
And blast the fig-tree that was only leaves?
And still the raging tumult of the seas?
Did He not bear the greatest pain of all,
Silent, upon the cross on Calvary?

REX BOUNDY

THE MAN OF GALILEE

He was no dreamer, dwelling in a cloud
    Of idle reason, strange philosophy;
In simple tasks His manhood strong He bowed
    Beneath hard toil and meager poverty.
Simple, not strange, the living words He saith—
The toiling Carpenter of Nazareth!

I cannot find Him, when, with fertile brain
    I ponder strange, amazing mystery;
But when my heart is darkened by the pain
    Of weariness or doubt or misery,
And someone smiles, or haply calls me friend,
    Or does a duty self-effacingly—
'Tis then His glowing face doth seem to bend
    Above me, and the living Christ I see—
    The Son of God, the Man of Galilee!

HILDEGARDE HOYT SWIFT

THE FAITH OF CHRIST'S FREEMEN

Our faith is not in dead saints' bones,
    In altars of vain sacrifice;
Nor is it in the stately stones
    That rise in beauty toward the skies.

Our faith is in the Christ who walks
    With men today, in street and mart;
The constant Friend who thinks and talks
    With those who seek Him with the heart.

We would not spurn the ancient lore,
    The prophet's word or psalmist's prayer;
But lo! our Leader goes before,
    Tomorrow's battles to prepare.

His Gospel calls for living men,
    With singing blood and minds alert;
Strong men, who fall to rise again,
    Who strive and bleed, with courage girt.

We serve no God whose work is done,
    Who rests within His firmament:
Our God, His labors but begun,
    Toils evermore, with power unspent.

God was and is and e'er shall be;
    Christ lived and loved—and loves us still;
And man goes forward, proud and free,
    God's present purpose to fulfill.

THOMAS CURTIS CLARK

FREEDOM

I am not strong till Thou hast clasped my hand,
I am not fit till by Thy side I stand.
I am not brave till Thou hast come to me;
Till Thou hast bound me fast, I am not free.

AUTHOR UNKNOWN

THERE'S ONE WILL LET ME IN

He taught me all the mercy, for he showed me all the sin.
Now, though my lamp was lighted late, there's One will
    let me in.

From The May Queen   ALFRED TENNYSON

THE DISCIPLE

I could not leave Thee, Christ! For when I tried
To leave Thee for alluring ways aside
From Thine own way, Thy power withheld me, kept
My feet from wandering too far, inept
And aimless, down a dwindling path that led
Through mazed confusion to the house of dread.

I could not leave Thee, Christ! For when I yearned
With passionate intensity and burned
With fiery torment to assuage my thirst
For freedom by a turbid stream that burst

In gushing torrents from a naked hill—
Thou ledst me back to waters deep and still.

I could not leave Thee, Christ! For when I sought
To fling aside Thy counsel, when I thought
That in my crazy freedom I should find
Some way of life for body, soul and mind
Better than Thou didst teach, I heard Thee say,
"Come back to Me, for thou hast lost thy way."

I would not leave Thee, Christ! For I am lame
From wandering, and the consuming flame
Of passion has gone out and left my soul
A smouldering ember, and the criss-crossed scroll
Of life ends as it started with the line,
"I cannot leave Thee, Christ! For I am Thine."

DWIGHT BRADLEY

IN PALESTINE

Have the rocks on the hillside voices—
    And the clods under trampling feet?
Do the cobblestones utter a message,
    And the pebbles tell secrets sweet?

Yes, the hills and the vales have voices,
    The rocks by the wayside speak:
They tell of the march of the ages,
    And of Him whom the nations seek.

GEORGE W. CARLIN

HAD CHRIST NOT LIVED AND DIED

Had Christ not lived, no temples to our God
Had proved His presence near:
Nor had stained glass revealed our Master dear,
More precious year by year;
Nor had the sculptor given our blessed Lord
The glorious lineaments that rank Him—Peer;
Nor had a Raphael on canvas stirred
The reader of God's Word
To homage of sweet Mary's Son, our Lord.

No reason could there be for Handel's art
To choose Messiah's name,
In themes inspired by love, no thought of fame,
A living, breathing flame,
Save that his genius touched the Sacred Heart,
So all encompassing in its acclaim:
Men bared their heads in life's too careless mart.
Remorse withdrew the cruel dart,
That pierced Christ Jesus pleading there apart.

EDITH LYNWOOD WINN

ROOM FOR HIM! ROOM!

Children of yesterday, heirs of tomorrow,
What are you weaving? Labor and sorrow?
Look to your looms again: Faster and faster
Fly the great shuttles prepared by the Master,
Life's in the loom: Room for it! Room!

Children of yesterday, heirs of tomorrow,
Lighten the labor and sweeten the sorrow;
Now, while the shuttles fly faster and faster,
Up, and be at it. At work with the Master.
He stands at your loom: Room for Him! Room!

Children of yesterday, heirs of tomorrow
Look at your fabric of labor and sorrow,
Seamy and dark with despair and disaster,
Turn it—and lo! The design of the Master.
The Lord's at the loom.
Room for Him! Room!

AUTHOR UNKNOWN

"HE CAME UNTO HIS OWN, AND HIS OWN RECEIVED HIM NOT"

As Christ the Lord was passing by,
He came, one night, to a cottage door,
He came, a poor man, to the poor;
He had no bed whereon to lie.

He asked in vain for a crust of bread,
Standing there in the frozen blast.
The door was locked and bolted fast.
"Only a beggar!" the poor man said.

Christ the Lord went further on,
Until He came to a palace gate.
There a king was keeping his state,
In every window the candles shone.

The king beheld Him out in the cold.
He left his guests in the banquet-hall.
He bade his servants tend them all.
"I wait on a Guest I know of old."

" 'Tis only a beggar-man!" they said.
"Yes," he said: "it is Christ the Lord."
He spoke to Him a kindly word,
He gave Him wine and he gave Him bread.

Now Christ is Lord of Heaven and Hell,
And all the words of Christ are true.
He touched the cottage, and it grew;
He touched the palace, and it fell.

The poor man is become a king.
Never was man so sad as he,
Sorrow and Sin on the throne make three,
He has no joy in mortal thing.

But the sun streams in at the cottage door
That stands where once the palace stood,
And the workman, toiling to earn his food
Was never a king before.

MARY ELIZABETH COLERIDGE

THE ARCHITECT

I would not call Him in, my heart decried
The use of any plans except my own;
By them I reared and ceiled four walls of stone.
As blindly too I shut myself inside.

No door was there, no casement opening wide
On darkness such as I had never known:
Imprisoned and discouraged and alone
I knelt amid the ruins of my pride.

And then He came, the Architect Divine,
In tenderness surpassing all my dreams.
"I am the Light," He said, "I am the door!"
On that I built anew this house of mine;
My walls became His windows, through them streams
The sunlight of His presence more and more.

MOLLY ANDERSON HALEY

FOLLOW ME

Lord, I would follow, but—
First, I would see what means that wondrous call
That peals so sweetly through Life's rainbow hall,
That thrills my heart with quivering golden chords,
And fills my soul with joys seraphical.

Lord, I would follow, but—
First, I would leave things straight before I go,—
Collect my dues, and pay the debts I owe;
Lest when I'm gone, and none is here to tend,
Time's ruthless hand my garnering o'erthrow.

Lord, I would follow, but—
First, I would see the end of this high road
That stretches straight before me, fair and broad;

So clear the way I cannot go astray,
It surely leads me equally to God.

Lord, I would follow,—yea,
Follow I *will*,—but first so much there is
That claims me in life's vast emergencies,—
Wrongs to be righted, great things to be done;
Shall I neglect these vital urgencies?

Who answers Christ's insistent call
Must give himself, his life, his all,
Without one backward look.
Who sets his hand unto the plow,
And glances back with anxious brow,
His calling hath mistook.
Christ claims him wholly for His own;
He must be Christ's and Christ's alone.

JOHN OXENHAM

THE SOUL'S NEED

The soul alone, like a neglected harp,
Grows out of tune, and needs a hand divine.
Dwell Thou within it, tune and touch the cords
Till every note and string shall answer Thine.
Abide in me! There have been moments pure
When I have seen Thy face and felt Thy power;
Then evil lost its grasp, and passion hushed.
Pulsed in the divine enchantment of the hour.

HARRIET BEECHER STOWE

TO THE CHRIST

Thou hast on earth a Trinity—
Thyself, my fellow-man, and me:
When one with him, then one with Thee:
Nor, save together, Thine are we.

JOHN B. TABB

LOVE

Love bade me welcome; yet my soul drew back,
    Guilty of dust and sin.
But quick-eyed Love, observing me grow slack
    From my first entrance in,
Drew nearer to me, sweetly questioning,
    If I lacked anything.

"A guest," I answered, "worthy to be here";
    Love said, "You shall be he."
"I, the unkind, ungrateful? Ah, my dear,
    I cannot look on Thee."
Love took my hand, and smiling, did reply,
    "Who made the eyes but I?"

"Truth, Lord, but I have marred them; let my shame
    Go where it doth deserve."
"And know you not," says Love, "Who bore the blame?"
    "My dear, then I will serve."
"You must sit down," says Love, "and taste My meat."
    So I did sit and eat.

GEORGE HERBERT

DISILLUSIONED

Through years our minds have wrestled—and how vain!—
With age-old doctrines, born of argument.
The years have left us bitter, spirit-spent.
For our stupendous toil, how little gain!
The Holy Word, which came to guide our way,
Has been an anvil for our mighty thought!
Its living truth, by suffering prophets bought,
Has long been lost amid the critics' fray.

How foolish we! O Man of Nazareth,
Who talked with peasants of the lily's charm,
Who took the little child upon Your arm,
Return and save us, Master, from this death.
Speak to our hearts, as once by Galilee,
And bid us, heavy-laden, follow Thee.

THOMAS CURTIS CLARK

THE INN OF LIFE

No room!
No room!
No room for Thee,
Thou Man of Galilee!
The house is full,
Yea, overfull.
There is no room for Thee,—
Pass on! Pass on!

Nay—see!
The place is packed.
We scarce have room
For our own selves.
So how shall we
Find room for Thee,
Thou Man of Galilee?—
    Pass on! Pass on!

But—if Thou shouldst
This way again,
And we can find
So much as one small corner
Free from guest,
Not then in vain
Thy quest.
But now—
The house is full.
Pass on!

Christ passes
On his ceaseless quest,
Nor will He rest
With any
Save as Chiefest Guest.

    *   *   *   *   *

Within my holy place
My Chiefest One is dwelling,
Not as a passing guest
But of His own houseling.
Oh, miracle of grace,
My whole heart's love compelling—

Within this tiny space
The Lord of All Good Life,
The Very Light of Life and Love
Is dwelling.

JOHN OXENHAM

SURRENDER

Oft in past days
I looked on Him, said lightly, "He is fair
Beyond all beauty Sharon's rose to wear;
Nor can the lily's grace with His compare;"
Then lightly went my ways.

But once He turned
On me a face so soiled—showed hands and feet
And side all wounded—whispered low and sweet,
"This was for thee!" Then in my veins the heat
Of worship's rapture burned.

Who could resist
Such utter fairness, fairer since so marred?
Or don chill mail of heedless disregard,
Seeing that brow which, lovelier since thorn-scarred,
Love's loveliness has kissed?

HENRY W. CLARK

ETERNAL CHRISTMAS

In the pure soul, although it sing or pray,
The Christ is born anew from day to day;
The life that knoweth Him shall bide apart
And keep eternal Christmas in the heart.

ELIZBETH STUART PHELPS

JUDEAN HILLS ARE HOLY

Judean hills are holy,
  Judean fields are fair,
For one can find the footprints
  Of Jesus everywhere.

One finds them in the twilight
  Beneath the singing sky,
Where shepherds watch in wonder
  White planets wheeling by.

His trails are on the hillsides
  And down the dales and deeps;
He walks the high horizons
  Where vesper silence sleeps.

He haunts the lowly highways
  Where human hopes have trod
The Via Dolorosa
  Up to the heart of God.

He looms, a lonely figure,
  Along the fringe of night,
As lonely as a cedar
  Against the lonely light.

Judean hills are holy,
  Judean fields are fair,
For one can find the footprints
  Of Jesus everywhere.

WILLIAM L. STIDGER

SYMBOL

My faith is all a doubtful thing,
    Wove on a doubtful loom,
Until there comes, each showery spring,
    A cherry tree in bloom;

And Christ, who died upon a tree
    That death had stricken bare,
Comes beautifully back to me,
    In blossoms everywhere.

DAVID MORTON

SACRAMENT

"His Body broken for your sake"—
I hear the words, and at the altar kneel,
And know that God is present here.
Into the sunlight from the fragrant dusk
I slowly pace, and see a world awry;
Crude, ugly buildings spawned by man;
Frustrate mortals searching out their hearts,
And finding dust and rottenness;
Hatred, malice, and a host of lesser, slimy sins . . .
And know that God is present here.

CATHERINE WILLIAMS HERZEL

CHRIST IN THE SOUL

Not the Christ in the manger,
Not the Christ on the cross,

But the Christ in the soul
Shall save that soul
When all but love is lost.

KATHARINE LEE BATES

From THE RING AND THE BOOK

No one ever plucked
A rag even, from the body of the Lord,
To wear and mock with, but despite himself
He looked the greater and was the better.

ROBERT BROWNING

THE MYSTICAL CHRIST

O Thou pale form!
Oft have I stood by Thee—
Have I been keeping lonely watch with Thee
In the damp night by weeping Olivet,
Or leaning on Thy bosom,
Or dying with Thee on the lonely cross,
Or witnessing Thy bursting from the tomb.

From Pauline   ROBERT BROWNING

WALLS

O Christ, they took Your living words
    And made from them a creed;
They built theology upon
    The words You meant to lead

Men through their darkness and their doubt
    Into a perfect light;
They made great walls that shut You out,
    And only shut in—night!

MYRIAM PAGE

VICTORY

To him that overcometh,
    John the Beloved said,
Is given the hidden manna
    To be his holy bread.

I drank Thy burning honey,
    Lord Jesus, long ago;
And still my heart goes hungry
    For all I do not know.

But, O my Lord, I thank Thee,
    I kiss Thy wounded feet;
To him that overcometh
    The common day is sweet!

MARGUERITE WILKINSON

UNDEFEATED

Out of the shame of my coward heart,
    Out of my night of defeat,
Lift me, O God, to the battle again,
    Cover my bitter retreat!

Out of despising my weakness and rout,
   Out of the love of Thy soul,
Purge me, O purge, with Thy hyssop, dear Christ,
   Give me my spirit made whole;

Beaten, but still undefeated, I pray
   Thou of unconquerable hand,
Reach me my poor broken saber again,
   I pledge Thee to die or to stand!

By the wonder of Heaven's forgiveness,
   By the lovely lure of Thy light,
By Thy spirit of victory eternal,
   God fling me again to the fight!

RALPH S. CUSHMAN

THE CROSS

The Cross is such a simple thing,
Yet of it men may talk and sing.

It is a ladder to the skies,
On which a mounting soul may rise.

It is a sign-board on the road,
To cheer man with his weary load.

It is a key that fits the door
To joyousness forevermore.

It signals to the human race
That God in mercy offers grace.

To some it is a stumbling block
That causes men to curse and mock;

To others who their sin bemoan
It can become a stepping stone.

To voyagers its sturdy form
Becomes an anchor in the storm.

A hammer, it has won renown
By battering old oppressions down.

Gripped by still others as a sword,
It has won battles for the Lord.

Dragged as a plowshare through the heart,
New furrows cause the grain to start.

It is a tree upon a hill
Whose fruit the hungry heart can fill.

It is a window for the soul;
'Tis medicine to make one whole.

The Cross is such a simple thing,
And yet it touches everything.

We cannot feel that such a sign
Is other than a power divine.

It is a beacon ever lit
By One identified with it.

CHARLES N. PACE

COME . . . LEARN!
GO . . . TEACH!

"Come—Learn!"
  So said my Lord to me!
And long I tarried in His school,
  That I His truth might see.

"Come—Learn!"
  I cried at length, "How long?"
And then with tenderness He said,
  "Till you learn strength and song!"

"Go—Teach!"
  Again His word came swift—
And I awoke from dreams to deeds,
  To tell men of His gift!

"Go—Teach!"
  And thus His love proclaim,
O'er earth and sea, to man and child,
  In every age the same!

"Learn—Teach!"
  The cycle endless is!
The more I learn, the more I teach;
  The glory ever His!

Ernest Bourner Allen

E TENEBRIS

Come down, O Christ, and help me! reach Thy hand,
For I am drowning in a stormier sea
Than Simon on the lake of Galilee:
The wine of life is spilt upon the sand,
My heart is as some famine-murdered land
Whence all good things have perished utterly,
And well I know my soul in Hell must lie
If I this night before God's throne should stand.
"He sleeps perchance, or rideth to the chase,
Like Baal, when his prophets howled that name
From morn to noon on Carmel's smitten height."
Nay, peace, I shall behold, before the night,
The feet of brass, the robe more white than flame,
The wounded hands, the weary human face.

OSCAR WILDE

CONSOLATOR

What shall we do when the great tides knock
And remorseless enter though walls be rock?
When the strong waves dash and the surges roll
And Creation's forces o'erwhelm the soul?
Christ! O Christ! once again say, "Peace!"
Yet once again bid the tempest cease!

What shall we do when the tides go back,
When the dull sky hangs over weed and wrack,
When there's nothing left for the dreary strand
But a foam-spread waste and a sea-wet sand?
Once again, O Christ! build Thy little fire;
Feed and comfort us, Heart's Desire!

MAI ELMENDORF LILLIE

From PROGRESS

Say ye: The spirit of man has found new roads,
　　And we must leave the old faiths, and walk therein?
Leave then the Cross as ye have left carved gods,
　　But guard the fire within!

Bright, else, and fast the stream of life may roll,
　　And no man may the other's hurt behold;
Yet each will have one anguish—his own soul
　　Which perishes of cold.

MATTHEW ARNOLD

EASTER SACRAMENTS

　　There is a Soul Gethsemane
　　　　Where I must kneel,
　　A prayer which I must pray
　　　　Till I can feel
　　That, though the anguish redden on my brow,
　　　　And Calvary's begun,
　　From him I'll take the sacrament of Love—
　　　　"Thy will, not mine, be done."

　　There is a Resurrection Life
　　　　That I must share,
　　A tomb that I must leave;
　　　　And though I bear

The wounds which I have won upon my cross,
Transfigured, they will shine—
A sacramental pledge of Love with Faith,
To make His rising mine.

HENRY PARK SCHAUFFLER

QUATRAIN

Christ bears a thousand crosses now
Where once but one He bore;
Each cruel deed unto His brow
Adds one thorn more.

CHARLES G. BLANDEN

CAESAR AND CHRIST

Proud Caesar came in strength of steel;
The panoply of war was his.
At his command men poured forth life,
The cities perished, nations fell.
He left as heritage a blood-stained tide;
He came, he scorned, he slaughtered—
And he died.

The meek Christ came, His strength the true—
A heart of love His panoply.
At His command men found their life,
The cities flourished, nations grew.
As heritage, the reign of peace He gives;
He came, He loved, He pitied—
And He lives.

THOMAS CURTIS CLARK

THE WHITE PRESENCE

Will not our hearts within us burn
    On the darkening road,
If a White Presence we can discern—
    Despite an ancient load?

Whither goest Thou, Pilgrim Friend?
    Lone Figure far ahead,
Wilt Thou not tarry until the end—
    And break our bread?

Follow we must amid sun or shade,
    Our faith to complete,
Journeying where no path is made—
    Save by His feet!

JOSEPH FORT NEWTON

THE NOBLER LESSON

Christ was of virgin birth, and, being slain,
The creedists say, He rose from death again.
Oh, futile age-long talk of death and birth!—
His life, that is the one thing wonder-worth;
Not how He came, but how He lived on earth.
For, if gods stoop, and with quaint jugglery
Mock nature's laws, how shall that profit thee!—
The nobler lesson is that mortals can
Grow godlike through this baffled front of man!

DON MARQUIS

AFTERNOON IN A CHURCH

I have grown tired of routine work
  And I have come to whisper a Name.
O, let men laugh and say I shirk,
  Beaten in the money game.

I hear a step; One comes to me
  And places His hand upon my head.
I feel the touch and I can see
  The finger tips are red.

His touch relieves the throbbing ache.
  He washes my tired and burning feet;
For He has been where crosses break,
  And comes here from the street.

RAYMOND KRESENSKY

MY GUIDE

There is no path in this desert waste;
  For the winds have swept the shifting sands,
The trail is blind where the storms have raced,
  And a stranger, I, in these fearsome lands.
But I journey on with a lightsome tread;
  I do not falter nor turn aside,
For I see His figure just ahead—
  He knows the way—my Guide.

There is no path in this trackless sea;
   No map is lined on the restless waves;
The ocean snares are strange to me
   Where the unseen wind in its fury raves.
But it matters naught; my sails are set,
   And my swift prow tosses the seas aside,
For the changeless stars are steadfast yet,
   And I sail by His star-blazed trail—my Guide.

There is no way in this starless night;
   There is naught but cloud in the inky skies;
The black night smothers me, left and right,
   I stare with a blind man's straining eyes.
But my steps are firm, for I cannot stray;
   The path to my feet seems light and wide;
For I hear His voice—"I am the Way!"
   And I sing as I follow Him on—my Guide.

ROBERT J. BURDETTE

COMPANIONSHIP

No distant Lord have I,
   Loving afar to be.
Made flesh for me He cannot rest
   Until He rests in me.

I need not journey far
   This dearest friend to see.
Companionship is always mine;
   He makes His home with me.

I envy not the twelve.
   Nearer to me is He.

The life He once lived here on earth
    He lives again in me.

Ascended now to God
    My witness there to be,
His witness here am I because
    His Spirit dwells in me.

O glorious Son of God,
    Incarnate Deity,
I shall forever be with Thee
    Because Thou art with me.

MALTBIE DAVENPORT BABCOCK

CONTEMPORARY

Then to "Emmaus" with Him I, too, walked.
No mark of nails in hands or feet I traced.
So quietly of star-wise dream He talked,
I did not know a Saviour with me paced
The dripping city street; that by my side,
In the familiar clothes of modern men,
There was rehearsed the tale of One who died
"To make earth good"; the thorns, the scourge again.

At lunch He told in simple phrase to me
The story of the strike and His arrest
Charged with inciting murder. A near tree
Bent while He talked of prison, Death for guest.
And when He spoke of rising from that tomb,
A cross of shadows slanted on the room.

SARA BARD FIELD

SANDALS

The Cross was black on Calvary,
  The Man hung lifeless now,
Unheeded lay the crown of thorns
  Upon His tortured brow.

We gambled for the clothes He wore,
  His sandals fell to me;
They had been scarred upon the road
  That winds to Calvary.

I clasped them on unholy feet,
  Set out upon my way—
The paths were strange the sandals chose,
  I could not make them stay:

They took me to an olive grove,
  So dark I could not see—
And I, who always scoffed at prayer,
  Knelt down beneath a tree.

They led me through a temple gate—
  And I, who claimed no soul,
Beheld a cripple kiss my feet
  And go his way, made whole.

They sought, and found, in Bethlehem,
  A stable, star-lit, bare—
An angel brushed me as I knelt
  Beside a manger there!

GOLDIE CAPERS SMITH

QUEST

I sought the face of Jesus
  In every crowded street,
I scanned each hurrying person
  A certain face to greet—
I thought, "The search is fruitless,
  And yet the Quest is sweet!"

I watched the toiling faces
  Of factory men at work,
I saw their souls reflected
  Through factory smoke and murk;
I saw grim prison faces
  Where strange emotions lurk.

I sought the face of Jesus
  In every child at play—
I watched for Him in women
  At market time each day;
I scanned the sad-eyed faces
  Along a silent way.

I found the smile of Jesus
  Upon a neighbour's face—
And in my mother's living
  I found His tender Grace,
Within the sick-room portal
  I saw His secret Place.

I saw the eyes of Jesus
  Within a motley throng,

I found the heart of Jesus
In a friendly heart and strong;
And heard the voice of Jesus
Within a singer's song!

DOROTHY TYRREL

THE COMING OF HIS FEET

In the crimson of the morning, in the whiteness of the noon,
In the amber glory of the day's retreat,
In the midnight, robed in darkness, of the gleaming of the
moon,
I listen for the coming of His feet.

I have heard His weary footsteps on the sands of Galilee,
On the temple's marble pavement, on the street,
Worn with weight of sorrow, faltering up the slopes of Cal-
vary,
The sorrow of the coming of His feet.

Down the minster-aisles of splendor, from betwixt the cher-
ubim,
Through the wondering throng, with motion strong and
fleet,
Sounds his victor tread, approaching with a music far and
dim—
The music of the coming of His feet.

Sandled not with sheen of silver, girdled not with woven
gold,
Weighted not with shimmering gems and odors sweet,
But white-winged and shod with glory in the Tabor-light
of old—
The glory of the coming of His feet.

He is coming, O my spirit, with His everlasting peace,
  With His blessedness immortal and complete,
He is coming, O my spirit, and His coming brings release.
  I listen for the coming of His feet.

LYMAN WHITNEY ALLEN

From THE HEALER

So stood of old the holy Christ
  Amidst the suffering throng;
With whom His lightest touch sufficed
  To make the weakest strong.

That healing gift He lends to them
  Who use it in His name;
The power that filled His garment's hem
  Is evermore the same.

That Good Physician liveth yet
  Thy friend and guide to be;
The Healer by Gennesaret
  Shall walk the rounds with thee.

JOHN GREENLEAF WHITTIER

THE LILIES OF THE FIELD

When I went up to Nazareth—
  A pilgrim of the spring—
When I went up to Nazareth
  The earth was blossoming!

I saw the blue flower of the flax
    Beside a shepherd's fold!
Along the hillsides' stony tracks
    I found the marigold!
The iris raised a shimmering spire
    Of beauty at my feet!
The poppy was a cup of fire
    Among the cooling wheat!

When I went up to Nazareth
    I marked how time came down
With blighting dust and withering **breath**
    Upon the hallowed town!
The years that buried Babylon
    Were drifting to efface
The steps of Mary's Heavenly Son,
    His dwelling and His face!
But still I read His permanence
    By signs that never dim;
With all their ancient eloquence
    The lilies spoke of Him!

DANIEL HENDERSON

AFRICA

I slept. I dreamed. I seemed to climb a hard, ascending track
And just behind me labored one whose face was black.
I pitied him, but hour by hour he gained upon my path.
He stood beside me, stood upright, and then I turned in
    wrath.
"Go back," I cried, "what right have you to stand beside
    me here?"
I paused, struck dumb with fear, for lo! the black man was
    not there—

But Christ stood in his place!
And oh! the pain, the pain, the pain that looked from that
dear face.

AUTHOR UNKNOWN

JESUS THE CHRIST

Our wars are wars of life, and wounds of love,
With intellect spears and long-winged arrows of thought,
Mutual, in one another's wrath, all renewing
We live as One Man. For contracting our infinite senses
We behold multitude; or expanding, we behold as One,
As one man all the Universal Family; and that man
We call Jesus the Christ, and He in us, and we in Him,
Live in perfect harmony in Eden the land of life,
Giving, receiving, and forgiving each other's trespasses.

From Before   ROBERT BROWNING

HOW HE CAME

When the golden evening gathered on the shore of Galilee,
When the fishing boats lay quiet by the sea,
Long ago the people wondered, tho' no sign was in the sky,
For the glory of the Lord was passing by.

Not in robes of purple splendor, not in silken softness shod,
But in raiment worn with travel came their God,
And the people knew His presence by the heart that ceased
to sigh
When the glory of the Lord was passing by.

For He healed their sick at even, and He cured the leper's
    sore,
And sinful men and women sinned no more,
And the world grew mirthful-hearted, and forgot its misery
When the glory of the Lord was passing by.

Not in robes of purple splendor, but in lives that do His will,
In patient acts of kindness He comes still;
And the people cry with wonder, tho' no sign is in the sky,
That the glory of the Lord is passing by.

                       W. J. DAWSON

"I AM THE WAY"

This is my faith in Thee,
  Tall Christ of Galilee,
Wherever I may be
  Thou art before—
Thou on the dizzying trail
  Thou in the shadowed vale,
Thou in the impassioned gale,
  Ever before.

Thou my soul's moving Guide,
  On with unwearying stride,
Morning and eventide,
  Ever before;
On with unhasted breath,
  Where my soul quivereth,
Into death, out of death,
  Ever before.

Thou my unwavering right,
    Thou my unbroken light,
Thou my unsullied White,
    Ever before.
This is my faith in Thee,
    Tall Christ of Galilee,
Wherever I may be,
    Thou art before.

ROBERT FREEMAN

PRAYER OF A MODERN THOMAS

If Thou, O God, the Christ didst leave,
In Him, not Thee, I do believe;
    To Jesus dying, all alone,
    To His dark Cross not Thy bright Throne,
My hopeless hands will cleave.

But if it was Thy love that died,
Thy voice that in the darkness cried,
    The print of nails I long to see,
    In Thy hands, God, who fashioned me,
Show me *Thy* piercèd side.

EDWARD SHILLITO

WE WOULD SEE JESUS

We would see Jesus! We would look upon
The light in that divinely human face,
Where lofty majesty and tender grace
    In blended beauty shone.

We would see Jesus, and would hear again
The voice that charmed the thousands by the sea,
Spoke peace to sinners, set the captives free,
    And eased the sufferers' pain.

We would see Jesus, yet not Him alone—
But see ourselves as in our Maker's plan;
And in the beauty of the Son of Man
    See man upon his throne.

We would see Jesus, and let Him impart
The truth He came among us to reveal,
Till in the gracious message we should feel
    The beating of God's heart.

W. J. Suckow

THEY TRIED TO TAKE YOU FROM ME

They tried to take You from me.
They said You were but an idle myth,
A delusion and a childish superstition;
When I prayed they mocked me,
And when I worshiped You they called me mad.
But O my Master—I have met You and I know!
I have heard You in the stillness of the night,
And in the infinite silence I have beheld Your glory;
In the hour of pain I have felt Your comforting hand.
How can I doubt You whom I know?

They tried to take You from me.
They proved in learned discourse that You never were;

They told me I was simple, and that You were but an
    empty dream;
Scientific proof they gave, and spoke wise words I could not
    understand;
They ridiculed and scoffed and laughed—
But O my Master—he that once has met You cannot
    doubt!
He that once has felt Your holy presence never questions
    more.
Though they are blind, yet have I seen Your splendor;
Though they are deaf, yet have I heard Your voice.
How can I doubt You whom I know?

CHURCHILL MURRAY

PRAYER

Great Master, touch us with Thy skillful hand;
Let not the music that is in us die!
Great Sculptor, hew and polish us; nor let,
Hidden and lost, Thy form within us lie!
Spare not the stroke. Do with us as Thou wilt.
Let there be naught unfinished, broken, marred.
Complete Thy purpose, that we may become
Thy perfect image, Thou our God and Lord.

HORATIO BONAR

CHRIST IN THE UNIVERSE

With this ambiguous earth
His dealings have been told us. These abide:
The signal to a maid, the human birth,
The lesson, and the young Man crucified.

But not a star of all
The innumerable host of stars has heard
How He administered this terrestrial ball.
Our race have kept their Lord's entrusted Word.

Of His earth-visiting feet
None knows the secret, cherished, perilous,
The terrible, shamefast, frightened, whispered, sweet,
Heart-shattering secret of His way with us.

No planet knows that this
Our wayside planet, carrying land and wave,
Love and life multiplied, and pain and bliss
Bears, as chief treasure, one forsaken grave.

Nor, in our little day,
May His devices with the heavens be guessed,
His pilgrimage to thread the Milky Way,
Or His bestowals there be manifest.

But in the eternities,
Doubtless we shall compare together, hear
A million alien Gospels, in what guise
He trod the Pleiades, the Lyre, the Bear.

O, be prepared, my soul!
To read the inconceivable, to scan
The million forms of God those stars unroll
When, in our turn, we show to them a Man.

ALICE MEYNELL

WESTMINSTER ABBEY

This great Cathedral seems to be
A pillared forest, dwarfing me.
The organ rolls a solemn note
From out a hidden chapel's throat;
And incense burns, and tapers gleam
Like mystic patterns in a dream.
But my loved Lord, oh, where is He?
Why does He hide His face from me?

This place is weary with the tears
And heartaches of unnumbered years.
Here lie the kings whose names are red
With bitter blood that they have shed.
How great, how great are wood and stone!
How small and frail are flesh and bone!
But in this place of kingly men
My Lord is not. Where is He then?

Oh, I have found Him otherwhere,
In little churches, still and fair.
But here my Lord could never stay
Where men come not to dream or pray.

MARIA CONDÉ

NOT MINE

It is not mine to run
    With eager feet
Along life's crowded ways,
    My Lord to meet.

It is not mine to pour
  The oil and wine
Or bring the purple robe
  And linen fine.

It is not mine to break
  At His dear feet
The alabaster box
  Of ointment sweet.

It is not mine to bear
  His heavy cross,
Or suffer, for His sake,
  All pain and loss.

It is not mine to walk
  Through valleys dim,
Or climb far mountain heights
  Alone with Him!

He hath no need of me
  In grand affairs,
Where fields are lost, or crowns
  Won, unawares.

Yet, Master, if I may
  Make one pale flower
Bloom brighter for Thy sake,
  Through one short hour;

If I, in harvest-fields
  Where strong ones reap,
May bind one golden sheaf
  For love to keep;

May speak one quiet word
   When all is still,
Helping some fainting heart
   To bear Thy will;

Or sing one high, clear song
   On which may soar
Some glad soul heavenward,
    I ask no more!

Julia C. R. Dorr

REQUESTS

I asked for Peace—
My sins arose,
And bound me close,
I could not find release.

I asked for Truth—
My doubts came in,
And with their din
They wearied all my youth.

I asked for Love—
My lovers failed.
And griefs assailed
Around, beneath, above.

I asked for Thee—
And Thou didst come
To take me home
Within Thy Heart to be.

D. M. Dolben

NEW DAY

Ere thou risest from thy bed,
Speak to God Whose wings were spread
O'er thee in the helpless night:
Lo, He wakes thee now with light!
Lift thy burden and thy care
In the mighty arms of prayer.

Lord, the newness of this day
Calls me to an untried way:
Let me gladly take the road,
Give me strength to bear my load,
Thou my guide and helper be—
I will travel through with Thee.

HENRY VAN DYKE

THE COMPANION

He found my house upon the hill,
  I made the bed and swept the floor,
And labored solitary, till
  He entered at the open door.

He sat with me to break my fast,
  He blessed the bread and poured the wine,
And spoke such friendly words, at last
  I knew not were they His or mine.

But only when He rose and went,
  And left the twilight in the door,
I found my hands were more content
  To make a bed and sweep a floor.

GERALD GOULD

THE RHYTHM OF HIS LIFE

Until I caught the rhythm of His life,
 I had not heard the music of the spheres,
The simple cadences of ancient psalms,
 The lyric beauty of a thousand years.

I had not seen the loveliness of dawn
 Across the lifted hills, the gold and gray
Of winter sunsets, or the moonlight's hush
 Upon a sleeping world, or flash of spray

Against eternal rocks! And now, behold!
 The Voiceless Future is a singing flame!
White Presences attend me everywhere,
 Their canticles an echo of His name!

MARY HALLET

I HAVE A LIFE IN CHRIST TO LIVE

I have a life in Christ to live;
 But ere I live it, must I wait
Till learning can clear answer give
 When asked of this or that book's date?

I have a life in Christ to live,
 A hope in Christ by which to die—
Must both await till science give
 To all my questions full reply?

AUTHOR UNKNOWN

MY YOKE IS EASY

The yokes He made were true.
Because the Man who dreamed
Was too
An artisan,
The burdens that the oxen drew
Were light.
At night
He lay upon his bed and knew
No beast of his stood chafing in a stall
Made restless by a needless gall.

The tenets of a man
May be full fine,
But if he fails with plumb and line,
Scorns care,
Smooth planing,
And precision with the square,
Some neck will bear
The scar of blundering!

GLADYS LATCHAW

O MASTER, LET ME WALK WITH THEE

O Master, let me walk with Thee
In lowly paths of service free;
Tell me Thy secret, help me bear
The strain of toil, the fret of care.

Help me the slow of heart to move
By some clear, winning word of love;
Teach me the wayward feet to stay,
And guide them in the homeward way.

Teach me Thy patience; still with Thee
In closer, dearer company,
In work that keeps faith sweet and strong,
In trust that triumphs over wrong,

In hope that sends a shining ray
Far down the future's broadening way,
In peace that only Thou canst give,
With Thee, O Master, let me live.

WASHINGTON GLADDEN

A RIVER OF GRACE

Make of my heart an upper room, I pray,
  Swept clean of pride, let self be but a door
Through which young lives may come to Thee this day
  To know Thee as they have not known before.

Speak through my voice that they may hear Thine own.
  Shine through my life in beauty and in truth
That they may see the Comrade Christ alone
  And in the glad impulsiveness of youth

Rise up as did those fisher-lads of Thine
  Who left their boats and nets to follow Thee,
So may they walk beside Thee, these of mine
  Whom out of all the world "Thou gavest me!"

MOLLY ANDERSON HALEY

THE WIDER LOVE

(To My Wife)

I would meet Christs on every avenue
 And hear each robin echo God's own throat
If I saw all as well as I see you
 And heard as clearly their essential note.

Universal love shall surely flower
 And hold us all as you and I each other.
I have no fears, not in this breathless hour,
 Aware that every woman is God's mother.

RALPH CHEYNEY

CHRIST IN WOOLWORTH'S

I did not think to find You there—
Crucifixes, large and small,
Sixpence and threepence, on a tray,
Among the artificial pearls,
Paste rings, tin watches, beads of glass.
It seemed so strange to find You there
Fingered by people coarse and crass,
Who had no reverence at all.
Yet—what is it that You would say?
"For these I hang upon My cross,
For these the agony and loss,
Though heedlessly they pass Me by."
Dear Lord, forgive such fools as I,
Who thought it strange to find You there,
When You are with us everywhere.

TERESA HOOLEY

DEDICATION FOR A HOME

O Thou whose gracious presence blest
   The home at Bethany,
This shelter from the world's unrest,
This home made ready for its Guest,
   We dedicate to Thee.

We build an altar here, and pray
   That Thou wilt show Thy face.
Dear Lord, if Thou wilt come to stay,
This home we consecrate today
   Will be a holy place.

JOHN OXENHAM

THE HOUSEWIFE

Jesus, teach me how to be
Proud of my simplicity.

Sweep the floors, wash the clothes,
Gather for each vase a rose.

Iron and mend a tiny frock,
Keeping one eye on the clock.

Always having time kept free
For childish questions asked of me.

Grant me wisdom Mary had
When she taught her little Lad.

CATHERINE CATE COBLENTZ

HYMN FOR A HOUSEHOLD

Lord Christ, beneath Thy starry dome
We light this flickering lamp of home,
And where bewildering shadows throng
Uplift our prayer and evensong.
Dost Thou, with heaven in thy ken
Seek still a dwelling-place with men,
Wandering the world in ceaseless quest?
O Man of Nazareth, be our guest!

Lord Christ, the bird his nest has found,
The fox is sheltered in his ground,
But dost Thou still this dark earth tread
And have no place to lay Thy head?
Shepherd of mortals, here behold
A little flock, a wayside fold
That wait thy presence to be blest—
O Man of Nazareth, be our guest!

DANIEL HENDERSON

PRAYER HYMN

Lord of all pots and pans and things, since I've no time to be
A Saint by doing lovely things, or watching late with Thee,
Or dreaming in the dawnlight, or storming Heaven's gates,
Make me a saint by getting meals, and washing up the
plates.

Although I must have Martha's hands, I have a Mary mind;
And when I black the boots and shoes, Thy sandals, Lord,
I find.

I think of how they trod the earth, what time I scrub the
    floor;
Accept this meditation, Lord, I haven't time for more.

Warm all the kitchen with Thy love, and light it with Thy
    peace;
Forgive me all my worrying, and make all grumbling cease.
Thou Who didst love to give men food, in room, or by the
    sea,
Accept this service that I do—I do it unto Thee.

M. K. H.

THE PASSWORD

When I shall come before Thy gate and stand
Knocking for entrance there, if Thou demand
That I should tell my faith, with head bent low,
I needs must answer, "Lord, I do not know,
Save that I held Love best;" to Thy demands
For count of what I did, my empty hands
Must bear sure witness that, of things I wrought,
Worthy the bringing I accomplished naught.

But this is foolishness. I hold no fear
That Thou wilt so demand. I shall draw near
Firm in my tread, and fling the portal wide,
Waiting no invitation. "Lord, I tried"
For all a Password, that my lips shall send
To meet Thine instant answer, "Pass, My friend."

Reginald C. Eva

MY MASTER'S FACE

No pictured likeness of my Lord have I;
He carved no record of His ministry
    On wood or stone.
He left no sculptured tomb nor parchment dim,
But trusted for all memory of Him
    Men's hearts alone.

Who sees the face but sees in part; who reads
The spirit which it hides, sees all; he needs
    No more. Thy grace—
Thy life in my life, Lord, give Thou to me;
And then, in truth, I may forever see
    My Master's face!

                WILLIAM HURD HILMER

SUBSTITUTION

When some beloved voice that was to you
Both sound and sweetness, faileth suddenly,
And silence against which you dare not cry,
Aches round you like a strong disease and new—
What hope? What help? What music will undo
That silence to your sense? Not friendship's sigh,
Not reason's subtle count; not melody
Of viols, nor of pipes that Faunus blew;
Not songs of poets, nor of nightingales.
Whose hearts leap upward through the cypress trees

To the clear moon; nor yet the spheric laws
Self-chanted, nor the angels' sweet "All-hails,"
Met in the smile of God: Nay, none of these,
Speak Thou, availing Christ!—and fill this pause.

ELIZABETH BARRETT BROWNING

FAILURE

I strove, O Lord, to grasp a star for Thee,
And, falling clutched the dust. "That bit of earth
Upon your palm is of a starry worth,"
I heard Thee say: "Give that instead to me!"

I thought in knightly quest or holy wars
To win Thee treasure. Bowed on a broken sword
I cried, "My hands are empty." Thou, O Lord,
Didst answer, "Nay, you bring a gift of scars."

Lord, I have sought Thy face in vain, and now
I weary. Ah, where art Thou? Hark! I hear
Thy voice: "You sought me, therefore I will wear
Your darkness as a light about my brow."

MARY SINTON LEITCH

CHRISTUS CONSOLATOR

Beside the dead I knelt for prayer,
    And felt a presence as I prayed.
Lo, it was Jesus standing there;
    He smiled: "Be not afraid!"

"Lord, Thou hast conquered death, we know;
 Restore again to life," I said,
"This one who died an hour ago."
 He smiled: "She is not dead."

"Asleep then, as Thyself didst say;
 Yet Thou canst lift the lids that keep
Her prisoned eyes from ours away;"
 He smiled: "She doth not sleep."

"Nay, then, though haply she do wake,
 And look upon some fairer dawn,
Restore her to our hearts that ache;"
 He smiled: "She is not gone."

"Alas; too well we know our loss,
 Nor hope again our joy to touch
Until the stream of death we cross."
 He smiled: "There is no such."

"Yet our beloved seem so far,
 The while we yearn to feel them near,
Albeit with Thee we trust they are."
 He smiled: "And I am here."

"Dear Lord, how shall we know that they
 Still walk unseen with us and Thee,
Nor sleep, nor wander far away?"
 He smiled: "Abide in Me."

ROSSITER W. RAYMOND

REVEALER OF THE FATHER

"The Heavens are telling the glory of God,"
  So sang the ancient bard.
    God is glorious.

"I believe in God the Father almighty,"
  Such is the theologian's creed.
    God is an almighty Father.

A Being who is infinite in wisdom and power,
  Is the contribution of the philosopher.
    God is infinite.

Omnipresent, omnipotent, everlasting—
  Still we are hungry to know
    What God is like.

Jesus understands and says,
  "He that hath seen Me hath seen the Father."
    God is like Christ.

    And we are satisfied.
                              ETNA DOOP-SMITH

IN GETHSEMANE

Dear Lord, how withered were the flowers
  Which in Gethsemane I trod;
How trampled in those midnight hours
  The Garden where I sought for God!

With selfish hands, O Christ, I came;
  Held sin's foul weight to press on Thee.
Enthralled by fears and secret shame,
  Thy bloody sweat I did not see.

Cold anguish clutched Thy heart divine;
  I too was bowed with sorrow there,
But only felt what grief was mine,
  Nor ever thought Thy pain to share.

These hands of mine relentless were;
  (Had fashioned Thine own agony);
Yet, when I held them forth in prayer,
  Thy hand it was that succored me!

CRAWFORD TROTTER

BARTIMEUS

God, grant to us Thy blessed Gift again,
To walk with us, as once in Galilee—
Talking of pebbles, and of birds o'erhead;
Of little children, and our daily bread—
To us, Thy lowly fisher-folk! Make plain
The shining wonder of Himself again
That we may touch the seamless garment's hem,
And be made whole of selfishness and sin;
Behold, the hearts made humble and contrite—
Lord, that we may at last receive our sight!

LAURA SIMMONS

DOUBT

O distant Christ, the crowded, darkening years
　Drift slow between Thy gracious face and me;
　My hungry heart leans back to look for Thee,
But finds the way set thick with doubts and fears.

My groping hands would touch Thy garment's hem,
　Would find some token Thou art walking near;
　Instead, they clasp but empty darkness drear,
And no diviner hands reach out to them.

Sometimes my listening soul, with bated breath,
　Stands still to catch a footfall by my side,
　Lest, haply, my earth-blinded eyes but hide
Thy stately figure, leading Life and Death;

My straining eyes, O Christ, but long to mark
　A shadow of Thy presence, dim and sweet,
　Or far-off light to guide my wandering feet,
Or hope for hands prayer-beating 'gainst the dark.

O Thou! unseen by me, that like a child
　Tries in the night to find its mother's heart,
　And weeping wanders only more apart,
Not knowing in the darkness that she smiled——

Thou, all unseen, dost hear my tired cry.
　As I, in darkness of a half-belief,
　Grope for Thy heart, in love and doubt and grief:
O Lord! speak soon to me—"Lo, here am I!"

MARGARET WADE DELAND

LO, I AM WITH YOU ALWAYS

Wide fields of corn along the valleys spread;
   The rain and dews mature the swelling vine;
I see the Lord in multiplying bread;
   I see Him turning water into wine;
   I see Him working all the works divine
He wrought when Salemward His steps were led;
   The selfsame miracles around Him shine;
He feeds the famished; He revives the dead;
   He pours the flood of light on darkened eyes;
He chases tears, diseases, fiends away;
   His throne is raised upon these orient skies;
His footstool is the pave whereon we pray.
   Ah, tell me not of Christ in Paradise,
For He is all around us here today.

JOHN CHARLES EARLE

I SEE HIS BLOOD UPON THE ROSE

I see His blood upon the rose
   And in the stars the glory of His eyes,
His Body gleams amid eternal snows,
   His tears fall from the skies.

I see His face in every flower;
   The thunder and the singing of the birds
Are but His voice—and carven by His power
   Rocks are His written words.

All pathways by His feet are worn,
  His strong heart stirs the ever-beating sea,
His crown of thorns is twined with every thorn,
  His cross is every tree.

JOSEPH MARY PLUNKETT

V

CRUSADE FOR CHRIST

PRAYER

White Captain of my soul, lead on;
I follow Thee, come dark or dawn.
Only vouchsafe three things I crave:
Where terror stalks, help me be brave!
Where righteous ones can scarce endure
The siren call, help me be pure!
Where vows grow dim, and men dare do
What once they scorned, help me be true!

ROBERT FREEMAN

WHERE ARE YOU GOING, GREAT-HEART?

Where are you going, Great-Heart,
With your eager face and your fiery grace?—
   Where are you going, Great-Heart?

"To fight a fight with all my might;
For Truth and Justice, God and Right;
To grace all Life and His fair Light."
   Then God go with you, Great-Heart!

Where are you going, Great-Heart?
"To live Today above the Past;
To make Tomorrow sure and fast;
To nail God's colors to the mast."
   Then God go with you, Great-Heart!

175

Where are you going, Great-Heart?
"To break down old dividing lines;
To carry out my Lord's designs;
To build again His broken shrines."
    Then God go with you, Great-Heart!

Where are you going, Great-Heart?
"To set all burdened peoples free;
To win for all God's liberty;
To 'stablish His Sweet Sovereignty."
    God goeth with you, Great-Heart!

JOHN OXENHAM

From BROTHERHOOD

There shall arise from this confused sound of voices
    A firmer faith than that our fathers knew,
A deep religion which alone rejoices
    In worship of the Infinitely true,
Not built on rite or portent, but a finer
And purer reverence for a Lord Diviner.

There shall come from out this noise of strife and groaning
    A broader and a juster brotherhood,
A deep equality of aim, postponing
    All selfish seeking to the general good.
There shall come a time when each shall to another
Be as Christ would have him—brother unto brother.

LEWIS MORRIS

THE SIGN OF THE SON OF MAN

Thy Kingdom, Lord, we long for,
  Where love shall find its own;
And brotherhood triumphant
  Our years of pride disown.
Thy captive people languish
  In mill and mart and mine;
We lift to Thee their anguish,
  We wait Thy promised Sign!

Thy Kingdom, Lord, Thy Kingdom!
  All secretly it grows;
In faithful hearts forever
  His seed the Sower sows;
Yet ere its consummation
  Must dawn a mighty doom;
For judgment and salvation
  The Son of Man shall come.

If now perchance in tumult
  His destined Sign appear,—
The rising of the people,—
  Dispel our coward fear!
Let comforts that we cherish,
  Let old traditions die,
Our wealth, our wisdom perish,
  So that He draw but nigh!

VIDA D. SCUDDER

THE SECOND CRUCIFIXION

Loud mockers in the roaring street
  Say Christ is crucified again:
Twice pierced His gospel-bearing feet,
  Twice broken His great heart in vain.

I hear and to myself I smile,
For Christ talks with me all the while.

No angel now to roll the stone
  From off his unawaking sleep,
In vain shall Mary watch alone,
  In vain the soldiers vigil keep.

Yet while they deem my Lord is dead
My eyes are on His shining head.

Ah! never more shall Mary hear
  That voice exceeding sweet and low
Within the garden calling clear:
  Her Lord is gone, and she must go.

Yet all the while my Lord I meet
In every London lane and street.

Poor Lazarus shall wait in vain,
  And Bartimeus still go blind;
The healing hem shall ne'er again
  Be touched by suffering humankind.

Yet all the while I see them rest,
The poor and outcast, on His breast.

No more unto the stubborn heart
    With gentle knocking shall He plead,
No more the mystic pity start,
    For Christ twice dead is dead indeed.

So in the street I hear men say,
Yet Christ is with me all the day.

RICHARD LE GALLIENNE

WHERE CROSS THE CROWDED WAYS OF LIFE

Where cross the crowded ways of life,
    Where sound the cries of race and clan,
Above the noise of selfish strife,
    We hear Thy voice, O Son of Man.

In haunts of wretchedness and need,
    On shadowed thresholds dark with fears,
From paths where hide the lures of greed,
    We catch the vision of Thy tears.

From tender childhood's helplessness,
    From woman's grief, man's burdened toil,
From famished souls, from sorrow's stress,
    Thy heart has never known recoil.

The cup of water given for Thee
    Still holds the freshness of Thy grace;
Yet long these multitudes to see
    The sweet compassion of Thy face.

O Master, from the mountain side,
　Make haste to heal these hearts of pain;
Among these restless throngs abide,
　O tread the city's streets again,

Till sons of men shall learn Thy love,
　And follow where Thy feet have trod;
Till glorious from Thy heaven above
　Shall come the City of our God.

FRANK MASON NORTH

LIVE CHRIST

Live Christ!—and though the way may be
　In this world's sight adversity,
He who doth heed thy every need
　Shall give thy soul prosperity.

Live Christ!—and though the road may be
　The narrow street of poverty,
He had not where to lay His head,
　Yet lived in largest liberty.

Live Christ!—and though the road may be
　The straight way of humility,
He who first trod that way of God
　Will clothe thee with His dignity.

Live Christ!—and though thy life may be
　In much a valedictory,
The heavy cross brings seeming loss,
　But wins the crown of victory.

Live Christ!—and all thy life shall be
A High Way of Delivery—
A Royal Road of goodly deeds,
Gold-paved with sweetest charity.

Live Christ!—and all thy life shall be
A sweet uplifting ministry,
A sowing of the fair white seeds
That fruit through all eternity.

JOHN OXENHAM

WHO WILL BUILD THE WORLD ANEW?

Who will build the world anew?
Who will break tradition's chains?
Who will smite the power of gold?
Who will chant the spirit's gains?

War and hatred, let them go!
Caste and creed have had their day;
Pride and lust will lose their power—
Who will find the better way?

Who will preach that might is weak?
Who will teach that love is power?
Who will hail the reign of right?
This his day and this his hour!

Faithless priests and warring lords
Are as Babylon and Tyre,
Making way for prophet hosts
Shouting truth in words of fire.

Who will live to slay the false?
Who will die to prove the true?
Who will claim the earth for God?
Who will build the world anew?

THOMAS CURTIS CLARK

FOR A NEW WORLD

God grant us wisdom in these coming days,
And eyes unsealed, that we clear visions see
Of that new world that He would have us build,
To life's ennoblement and His high ministry.

God give us sense—God-sense, of life's new needs,
And souls aflame with new-born chivalries—
To cope with those black growths that foul the ways—
To cleanse our poisoned founts with God-born energies.

To pledge our souls to nobler, loftier life,
To win the world to His fair sanctities,
To bind the nations in a pact of peace,
To free the soul of life for finer loyalties.

Not since Christ died upon His lonely cross
Has time such prospect held of life's new birth;
Not since the world of chaos first was born
Has man so clearly visaged hope of a new earth.

Not of our own might can we hope to rise
Above the ruts and failures of the past.
But with His help who did the first earth build,
With hearts courageous we may fairer build this last.

JOHN OXENHAM

DAY DAWN OF THE HEART

'Tis not enough that Christ was born
  Beneath the star that shone,
And earth was set that holy morn
  Within a golden zone.
He must be born within the heart
  Before He finds His throne,
And brings the day of love and good,
The reign of Christlike brotherhood.

MARY T. LATHROP

THE UNIVERSAL LANGUAGE

The wise men ask, "What language did Christ speak?"
  They cavil, argue, search, and little prove,
O Sages, leave your Syriac and your Greek!
  Christ spoke the universal language—Love.

ELLA WHEELER WILCOX

A PARABLE

Said Christ our Lord, "I will go and see
How the men, my brethren, believe in Me."
He passed not again through the gate of birth,
But made Himself known to the children of earth.

Then said the chief priests, and rulers, and kings,
"Behold, now, the Giver of all good things;

Go to, let us welcome with pomp and state
Him who alone is mighty and great."

With carpets of gold the ground they spread
Wherever the Son of Man should tread,
And in palace chambers lofty and rare
They lodged Him, and served Him with kingly fare.

Great organs surged through arches dim
Their jubilant floods in praise of Him;
And in church, and palace, and judgment-hall,
He saw His image high over all.

But still, wherever his steps they led,
The Lord in sorrow bent down His head,
And from under the heavy foundation-stones
The son of Mary heard bitter groans.

And in church, and palace, and judgment-hall,
He marked great fissures that rent the wall,
And opened wider and yet more wide
As the living foundation heaved and sighed.

"Have ye founded your thrones and altars, then,
On the bodies and souls of living men?
And think ye that building shall endure,
Which shelters the noble and crushes the poor?

"With gates of silver and bars of gold
Ye have fenced my sheep from their Father's fold;
I have heard the dropping of their tears
In heaven these eighteen hundred years."

"O Lord and Master, not ours the guilt,
We build but as our fathers built;
Behold Thine images, how they stand,
Sovereign and sole, through all our land.

"Our task is hard—with sword and flame
To hold Thine earth forever the same,
And with sharp crooks of steel to keep
Still, as Thou leftest them, Thy sheep."

Then Christ sought out an artisan,
A low-browed, stunted, haggard man,
And a motherless girl, whose fingers thin
Pushed from her faintly want and sin.

Them set He in the midst of them,
And as they drew back their garment-hem,
For fear of defilement, "Lo, here," said He,
"The images ye have made of Me!"

JAMES RUSSELL LOWELL

MAKE THE WORLD A HOME

Oh, come, ye toilers of the earth,
   Ye who for masters sow and reap,
Who make and dye, but have no cloth,
   Whose fruits are but the tears ye weep.

Come, ye who build but homeless are,
   Who are as cattle bought and sold,

Whose souls and bodies are but grist,
    Your children too, but ground to gold.

Oh, come, ye outcasts of the earth,
    And let us end the human night,
The priests and masters, yokes and lies,
    And build for love the world of light.

Oh, piteous procession, come,
    Yoke-bearers of the human night,
And let us make the world a home,
    A fellowship of love and light.

GEORGE D. HERRON

"HIS THRONE IS WITH THE OUTCAST"

I followed where they led,
    And in a hovel rude,
With naught to fence the weather from His head,
    The King I sought for meekly stood;
A naked hungry child
    Clung round His gracious knee,
And a poor hunted slave looked up and smiled
    To bless the smile that set him free;
New miracles I saw His presence do,
    No more I knew the hovel bare and poor,
The gathered chips into a woodpile grew
    The broken morsel swelled to goodly store.
I knelt and wept: my Christ no more I seek.
His throne is with the outcast and the weak.

J. R. LOWELL

IF HE SHOULD COME

If Jesus should tramp the streets tonight,
    Storm-beaten and hungry for bread,
Seeking a room and a candle light
    And a clean though humble bed,
Who would welcome the Workman in,
    Though He came with panting breath,
His hands all bruised and His garments thin—
    This Workman from Nazareth?

Would rich folk hurry to bind His bruise
    And shelter His stricken form?
Would they take God in with His muddy shoes
    Out of the pitiless storm?
Are they not too busy wreathing their flowers
    Or heaping their golden store—
Too busy chasing the bubble hours
    For the poor man's God at the door?

And if He should come where churchmen bow,
    Forgetting the greater sin,
Would He pause with a light on His wounded brow,
    Would He turn and enter in?
And what would He think of their creeds so dim,
    Of their weak, uplifted hands,
Of their selfish prayers going up to Him
    Out of a thousand lands?

EDWIN MARKHAM

THE WAY

Pass not too near these outcast sons of men
Where walked your Christ ahead! lest you, too, share
The rabble's wrath! in time take heed! beware
The woe—the bitter shame of Him again!
Your flaming zeal speak not so rash—so loud!
Keep on your prudent way within the crowd!

What if they mark you of His band, and cry:
"Behold this one, as well!" ah, you should know
The jeers, the stones, for all that with Him go!
Have caution, fool! let others yearn and die;
These broken ones you love with hot heartbreak
Can save you not! Be warned by His mistake.
Remember how He spurned the risk and loss!
Remember how they nailed Him to a Cross!

LAURA SIMMONS

TO A STUDENT

Let crowded city pavements be your school;
    Your text, the varied faces that you see;
An understanding heart and mind, your tool;
    The art of human kindness your degree.

E. K. BIDDLE

EARTH IS ENOUGH

We men of earth have here the stuff
Of Paradise—we have enough!

We need no other stones to build
The Temple of the Unfulfilled—
No other ivory for the doors—
No other marble for the floors—
No other cedar for the beam
And dome of man's immortal dream.
Here on the paths of every-day,
Here on the common human way,
Is all the stuff the gods would take
To build a Heaven, to mold and make
New Edens. Ours the task sublime
To build Eternity in time!

EDWIN MARKHAM

From THE VISION OF SIR LAUNFAL

And the voice that was softer than silence said,
"Lo it is I, be not afraid!
In many climes, without avail,
Thou hast spent thy life for the Holy Grail;
Behold, it is here,—this cup which thou
Didst fill at the streamlet for Me but now;
This crust is My body broken for thee,
This water His blood that died on the tree;
The Holy Supper is kept, indeed,
In whatso we share with another's need;
Not what we give, but what we share,
For the gift without the giver is bare;
Who gives himself with his alms feeds three,
Himself, his hungering neighbor, and Me."

JAMES RUSSELL LOWELL

CREED AND DEED

What care I for caste or creed?
It is the deed, it is the deed;
What for class or what for clan?
It is the man, it is the man;
Heirs of love, and joy, and woe,
Who is high, and who is low?
Mountain, valley, sky, and sea,
Are for all humanity.

What care I for robe or stole?
It is the soul, it is the soul;
What for crown, or what for crest?
It is the heart within the breast;
It is the faith, it is the hope,
It is the struggle up the slope,
It is the brain and eye to see,
One God and one humanity.

ROBERT LOVEMAN

BROTHERHOOD

God, what a world, if men in street and mart
Felt that same kinship of the human heart
Which makes them, in the face of fire and flood,
Rise to the meaning of True Brotherhood.

ELLA WHEELER WILCOX

TO DREAMERS EVERYWHERE

And if your own and time alike betray you,
If all you hoped and wrought for does not come,
Why should that dismay you?
Why should creeping doubt benumb
The leaping pulses of your will?
Have patience and be strong.
Seems your waiting long?
One has waited longer, who is waiting still.

AMELIA JOSEPHINE BURR

"HE THAT DOETH THE WILL"

From all vain pomps and shows,
From the pride that overflows,
And the false conceits of men;
From all the narrow rules
And subtleties of Schools,
And the craft of tongue and pen;
Bewildered in its search,
Bewildered with the cry:
Lo, here! lo, there, the Church!
Poor, sad Humanity
Through all the dust and heat
Turns back with bleeding feet,
By the weary road it came,
Unto the simple thought
By the great Master taught,
And that remaineth still:
Not he that repeateth the name,
But he that doeth the will!

From Christus   HENRY WADSWORTH LONGFELLOW

THE NEW PATRIOT

Who is the patriot? he who lights
  The torch of war from hill to hill?
Or he who kindles on the heights
  The beacon of a world's good will?

Who is the patriot? he who sends
  A boastful challenge o'er the sea?
Or he who sows the earth with friends,
  And reaps world-wide fraternity?

Who is the patriot? It is he
  Who knows no boundary, race or creed,
Whose nation is humanity,
  Whose countrymen all souls that need;

Whose first allegiance is vowed
  To the fair land that gave him birth,
Yet serves among the doubting crowd
  The broader interests of the earth.

The soil that bred the pioneers
  He loves and guards, yet loves the more
That larger land without frontiers,
  Those wider seas without a shore.

Who is the patriot? Only he
  Whose business is the general good,
Whose keenest sword is sympathy,
  Whose dearest flag is brotherhood.

FREDERICK LAWRENCE KNOWLES

FORGIVE

Forgive, O Lord, our severing ways,
The rival altars that we raise,
The wrangling tongues that mar Thy praise!

Thy grace impart! In time to be
Shall one great temple rise to Thee—
Thy Church our broad humanity.

White flowers of love its walls shall climb,
Soft bells of peace shall ring its chime,
Its days shall all be holy time.

A sweeter song shall then be heard,
Confessing, in a world's accord,
The inward Christ, the living Word.

That song shall swell from shore to shore.
One hope, one faith, one love restore
The seamless robe that Jesus wore.

JOHN GREENLEAF WHITTIER

"WE HAVE SEEN HIS STAR IN THE EAST"

"We have seen His star in the East,"
    In the East where it first stood still,
We have heard the song of the angel throng,
    "And on earth peace, good will!"

But the little lights confuse,
  The nearer sounds obsess,
And our hearts withhold from the Lord of Love
  The lives He would use and bless.

"We have seen His star in the East,"
  His shining dream of the good,
When men shall claim in the Father's name
  Their right to brotherhood.
O little lights, grow dim,
  O nearer sounds, be still,
While our hearts remember Bethlehem,
  And a cross on a far green hill!"

MOLLY ANDERSON HALEY

IS THIS THE TIME TO HALT?

Is this the time, O Church of Christ! to sound
Retreat? To arm with weapons cheap and blunt
The men and women who have borne the brunt
Of truth's fierce strife, and nobly held their ground?
Is this the time to halt, when all around
Horizons lift, new destinies confront,
Stern duties wait our nation, never wont
To play the laggard, when God's will was found?

No! rather, strengthen stakes and lengthen cords,
Enlarge thy plans and gifts, O thou elect,
And to thy kingdom come for such a time!
The earth with all its fullness is the Lord's.
Great things attempt for Him, great things expect,
Whose love imperial is, whose power sublime.

CHARLES SUMNER HOYT

SOUL-FEEDING HYACINTHS

Be with us, Lord, today,
And set us free
From foolish bickerings,
From cant and pettiness, the ugly things
That keep us less
Than Thou wouldst have us be;
Open our eyes that we may see
The Vision Beautiful,
And if we are enmeshed
In dreary labyrinths of everyday,
Grant us release,
And give us peace, O Lord;
An understanding sure and swift,
The very precious gift
Of loving insight. Help us to change
The bread and butter of monotony
Into soul-feeding hyacinths,
Fragrant with service; and until we take
The noblest, highest, truest way,
Let us not rest content;
And of our fellowship today
Help us to make
A joyous sacrament.

CORINNE FARLEY

THUS SPEAKETH CHRIST OUR LORD

Ye call Me Master and obey Me not,
Ye call Me Light and see Me not,

Ye call Me Way and walk not,
Ye call Me Life and desire Me not,
Ye call Me wise and follow Me not,
Ye call Me fair and love Me not,
Ye call Me rich and ask Me not,
Ye call Me eternal and seek Me not,
Ye call Me gracious and trust Me not,
Ye call Me noble and serve Me not
Ye call Me mighty and honor Me not,
Ye call Me just and fear Me not;
If I condemn you, blame Me not.

[Engraved on an old slab in the Cathedral of Lübeck, Germany.]

INDIFFERENCE

When Jesus came to Golgotha they hanged Him on a tree,
They drave great nails through hands and feet, and made a
    Calvary;
They crowned Him with a crown of thorns, red were His
    wounds and deep,
For those were crude and cruel days, and human flesh was
    cheap.

When Jesus came to Birmingham, they simply passed Him
    by,
They never hurt a hair of Him, they only let Him die;
For men had grown more tender, and they would not give
    Him pain,
They only just passed down the street, and left Him in the
    rain.

Still Jesus cried, "Forgive them for they know not what
    they do,"
And still it rained the winter rain that drenched Him
    through and through;
The crowds went home and left the streets without a soul
    to see,
And Jesus crouched against a wall and cried for Calvary.

G. A. STUDDERT KENNEDY

HE WORKED

He worked! It is enough
That His own hands were
Tarnished with the stuff.
He knew the law's demands
For daily bread, the tasks,
The toils, the rude tools of His day;
The sweating face; nor did He ask,
In all his time, an easier way.

With hammer, saw and awkward wrench,
He proved Himself the man.
Though Spirit-born, by the rude bench
He joined our race and ran
Its rugged course to where it ends.
While of a holier life He taught,
To which the soul ascends,
He lived, He wept, He wrought
With us—He called us friends.

J. N. SCHOLES

CARPENTER CHRIST

Carpenter Christ, I know that You must understand. I
    praise You most for work.
Surely hands that stripped the cedar bough in Nazareth must
    be akin to hands that love the homely touch of bread.
Surely fingers that had no fear to heal the leper must know
    the joy of menial tasks to rest a weary one.
And eyes that watched a passion flower triumphant on a
    barren hill must live again to see the ecstasy of every
    living bloom.
Carpenter Christ!

MILDRED FOWLER FIELD

CERTAINTIES

In all His life and teaching
    But two sure things we find,
Two certainties far-reaching:
    He suffered and was kind.

The wounded Christs are falling
    In village and in street
Of miseries appalling,
    With bleeding hearts and feet.

"Where is the kindly Jesus,"
    Their anguished voices say,
"Whose healing touch will ease us
    And take our grief away?"

When shall we cease to cherish
   Christ arrogant on high
And turn to those that perish,
   To him about to die?

God's children faint and sicken,
   With gall their cup is spiced.
Make us, to help these stricken,
   Each one a kindly Christ!

KENNETH W. PORTER

MARY'S SON

Jesus, the friend of lonely, beaten folk,
   Comrade, defender of each humble one,
Who put Your generous shoulders to the yoke
   That we might live in nobler unison,

Why have we worshiped You with sword and flame,
   Placed You, a worker, on a regal throne
And let our brothers' blood flow in Your name,
   Who loved all human creatures as Your own?

Let us remember You as Mary's son,
   A worker, seeking rights for men who toil,
Conscious that we are brothers every one
   Upon the glowing earth's fraternal soil.

Let us remember You as one who died
For love of every comrade at His side.

LUCIA TRENT

THE TRIMMED LAMP

I dare not slight the stranger at my door—
    Threadbare of garb and sorrowful of lot—
Lest it be Christ that stands; and goes His way
    Because I, all unworthy, knew Him not.

I dare not miss one flash of kindling cheer
    From alien souls, in challenge glad and high.
Ah, what if God be moving very near
    And I, so blind, so deaf, had passed Him by?

LAURA SIMMONS

AS YE DO IT UNTO THESE

In little faces pinched with cold and hunger
Look, lest ye miss Him! In the wistful eyes,
And on the mouths unfed by mother kisses,
Marred, bruised and stained His precious image lies!
And when ye find Him in the midnight wild,
Even in the likeness of an outcast child,
O wise men, own your King!
Before his cradle bring
Your gold to raise and bless,
Your myrrh of tenderness,
For, "As ye do it unto these," said He,
"Ye do it unto Me."

AUTHOR UNKNOWN

WHAT DO I OWE?

What do I owe?
    Nay, Lord—what do I not?
—All that I am,
    And all that I have got;—
All that I am,
    And that how small a thing,
Compared with all
    Thy goodly fostering.

What do I owe
    To those who follow on?
—To build more sure
    The Freedom we have won;—
To build more sure,
    The Kingdoms of Thy Grace,
Kingdoms secure
    In Truth and Righteousness.

What do I owe
    To Christ, my Lord, my King?
That all my life
    Be one sweet offering;—
That all my life
    To noblest heights aspire,
That all I do
    Be touched with holy fire.

JOHN OXENHAM

THE SPIRIT OF YOUTH

Nobly our sires have striven
  In their God-given day;
Faithfully have they followed
  What light illumed their way.
Now, with new dreams, forgetting
  Days that are past and dead,
God grant we may not falter
  In the new tasks ahead!

War is a ghastly specter,
  Haunting this age of peace;
Yet shall our ranks go forward
  Seeking the world's release—
Freedom from greed and plunder,
  Freedom from pride and hate.
God give us strength and wisdom
  For the new tasks of state!

Love be the lore for our learning;
  Justice and right, our cry;
God's kingdom come! our slogan,
  As the good days draw nigh.
Let no man shame our courage,
  Let none despise our youth—
Making the old world over
  After the ways of truth!

Thomas Curtis Clark

JESUS CHRIST—AND WE

Christ has no hands but our hands
 To do His work today;
He has no feet but our feet
 To lead men in His way;
He has no tongue but our tongues
 To tell men how He died;
He has no help but our help
 To bring them to His side.

We are the only Bible
 The careless world will read;
We are the sinner's gospel,
 We are the scoffer's creed;
We are the Lord's last message
 Given in deed and word—
What if the line is crooked?
 What if the type is blurred?

What if our hands are busy
 With other work than His?
What if our feet are walking
 Where sin's allurement is?
What if our tongues are speaking
 Of things His lips would spurn?
How can we hope to help Him
 Unless from Him we learn?

ANNIE JOHNSON FLINT

I SHALL NOT PASS AGAIN THIS WAY

The bread that bringeth strength I want to give,
The water pure that bids the thirsty live:
I want to help the fainting day by day;
I'm sure I shall not pass again this way.

I want to give the oil of joy for tears,
The faith to conquer crowding doubts and fears.
Beauty for ashes may I give alway:
I'm sure I shall not pass again this way.

I want to give good measure running o'er,
And into angry hearts I want to pour
The answer soft that turneth wrath away;
I'm sure I shall not pass again this way.

I want to give to others hope and faith,
I want to do all that the Master saith;
I want to live aright from day to day;
I'm sure I shall not pass again this way.

AUTHOR UNKNOWN

OTHERS

Lord, help me live from day to day
In such a self-forgetful way
That even when I kneel to pray
My prayers will be for OTHERS.

Help me in all the work I do
  To ever be sincere and true
And know that all I do for You
  Must needs be done for OTHERS.

Let Self be crucified and slain
  And buried deep, and all in vain
May efforts be to rise again
  Unless to live for OTHERS.

And when my work on earth is done
  And my new work in heaven begun
May I forget the crown I've won
  While thinking still of OTHERS.

Others, Lord, yes, others
  Let this my motto be;
Help me to live for Others
  That I may live like Thee.

CHARLES D. MEIGS

THE TORCH BEARER

The God of High Endeavor
  Gave me a torch to bear.
I lifted it high above me
  In the dark and murky air;
And straightway with loud hosannas
  The crowd proclaimed its light
And followed me as I carried my torch
  Through the starless night,
Till drunk with the people's praises
  And mad with vanity

I forgot 'twas the torch that they followed
   And fancied they followed me.

Then slowly my arm grew weary
   Upholding the shining load
And my tired feet went stumbling
   Over the dusty road.
And I fell with the torch beneath me.
   In a moment the light was out.
When lo! from the throng a stripling
   Sprang forth with a mighty shout,
Caught up the torch as it smoldered
   And lifted it high again,
Till fanned by the winds of heaven
   It fired the souls of men.

And as I lay in the darkness
   The feet of the trampling crowd
Passed over and far beyond me,
   Its pæans proclaimed aloud,
And I learned in the deepening twilight
   The glorious verity,
'Tis the torch that the people follow,
   Whoever the bearer may be.

AUTHOR UNKNOWN

I KNOW A NAME

I know a soul that is steeped in sin,
   That no man's art can cure;
But I know a Name, a Name, a Name,
   That can make that soul all pure.

I know a life that is lost to God,
  Bound down by things of earth;
But I know a Name, a Name, a Name,
  That can bring that soul new birth.

I know of lands that are sunk in shame,
  Of hearts that faint and tire;
But I know a Name, a Name, a Name,
  That can set those lands on fire.
Its sound is a brand, its letters flame,
I know a Name, a Name, a Name,
  That will set those lands on fire.

AUTHOR UNKNOWN

From CHRIST OF THE ANDES

"Christ of the Andes," Christ of Everywhere,
Great Lover of the hills, the open air,
And patient Lover of impatient men
Who blindly strive and sin and strive again.
Thou Living Word, larger than any creed,
Thou Love Divine, uttered in human need—
Oh, teach the world, warring and wandering still,
The way of Peace, the footpath of Good Will.

HENRY VAN DYKE

THE CARPENTER

I wonder what He charged for chairs at Nazareth.
And did men try to beat Him down

And boast about it in the town—
"I bought it cheap for half-a-crown
From that mad Carpenter?"

And did they promise and not pay,
Put it off to another day;
O, did they break His heart that way,
My Lord, the Carpenter?

I wonder did He have bad debts,
And did He know my fears and frets?
The gospel writer here forgets
To tell about the Carpenter.

But that's just what I want to know.
Ah! Christ in glory, here below
Men cheat and lie to one another so;
It's hard to be a carpenter.

G. A. Studdert Kennedy

A FOLLOWER

I might have climbed up Calvary
    With willing steps, though slow,
And found the way less steep to me
    Than feet reluctant know.

I might have held the cooling cup
    To lips grown gray with pain,
And in the act of looking up
    Known agony as gain.

Instead, I feel myself to be,
  Through shame and conscious loss,
One Simon of Cyrene—
  Compelled to bear my cross.

DAISY CONWAY PRICE

HYMN

O patient Christ! when long ago
  O'er old Judea's rugged hills
Thy willing feet went to and fro,
  To find and comfort human ills—
    Did once Thy tender, earnest eyes,
    Look down the solemn centuries,
    And see the smallness of our lives?

Souls struggling for the victory,
  And martyrs, finding death was gain,
Souls turning from the Truth and Thee,
  And falling deep in sin and pain—
    Great heights and depths were surely seen,
    But oh! the dreary waste between—
    Small lives, not base perhaps, but mean:

Their selfish efforts for the right,
  Or cowardice that keeps from sin——
Content to only see the height
  That nobler souls will toil to win!
    Oh, shame, to think Thine eyes should see
    The souls contented just to be—
    The lives too small to take in Thee.

Lord, let this thought awake our shame,
  That blessed shame that stings to life,
Rouse us to live for Thy dear name.
  Arm us with courage for the strife.
    O Christ! be patient with us still;
      Dear Christ! remember Calvary's hill—
    Our little lives with purpose fill!

MARGARET WADE DELAND

THE CHRISTMAS TREE

If Christ could ever be born again,
  Who would His Mother be?
"I," said Sorrow; and "I," said Pain;
  And "I," said Poverty.

But how, were Christ so made again,
  Could one be born of Three?
"Are not the griefs of earth a strain
  Of the Blessed Trinity?"

And who, on His birth-night, again
  His worshipers would be?
"Love," said Sorrow; and "Pity," said Pain;
  And "Peace," said Poverty.

And who the seers, from what strange lands,
  Would come to look at Him?
"The simple and wise, with serving hands,
  And little ones light of limb."

And what would the kings of earth do then?
   "Put simple and wise to flight;
While loud in the darkened homes of men
   Little ones cried for light."

What use, what use, if once again
   The world rejects the Sign?
"Christ will still be a Lover of men,
   And His heart may be yours and mine.

"For this is the Tree whose blessed yield
   Bears seed in darkest ground;
And a wound by those bright leaves is healed,
   Wherever a wound is found."

Edward Shillito

THE CARPENTER

Silent at Joseph's side He stood,
And smoothed and trimmed the shapeless wood.
And with firm hand, assured and slow,
Drove in each nail with measured blow.

Absorbed, He planned a wooden cask,
Nor asked for any greater task.
Content to make, with humble tools,
Tables and little children's stools.

Lord, give me careful hands to make
Such simple things as for Thy sake.
Happy within Thine House to dwell
If I may make one table well.

Phyllis Hartnoll

CROSSES

Crosses for Light, crosses for Love!
   This is the dirge that life will bring.
Crosses for Light, crosses for Love,
   And the newest cross, an old, old thing.

They who pass in the shining way
   With passion for others, and grief for pay,
Measure their steps by a bitter lay—
   "Crosses for Light and Love"—alway.

New the wood, and nailed to stay,
   The hill before one all the way,
But the dirge of that long-time yesterday
   Is the marching song of men today.

                      Edward Williams

FROM NAZARETH

Comes any good from Nazareth?
   The scornful challenge as of old
Is flung on many a jeering breath
   From cloistered cells and marts of gold.

Comes any good from Nazareth?
   Behold, the mighty Nazarene,
The Lord of life, the Lord of death,
   Through warring ages walks serene.

One touch upon His garment's fringe
   Still heals the hurt of bitter years.

Before Him yet the demons cringe,
   He gives the wine of joy for tears.

O city of the Carpenter,
   Upon the hill slope old and gray,
The world amid its pain and stir
   Turns yearning eyes on thee today.

For He who dwelt in Nazareth,
   And wrought with toil of hand and brain,
Alone gives victory to faith
   Until the day He comes again.

MARGARET E. SANGSTER

CRUCIFIXION

"Lord, must I bear the whole of it, or none?"
"Even as I was crucified, My son."

"Will it suffice if I the thorn-crown wear?"
"To take the scourge, My shoulders were made bare."

"My hands, O Lord, must I be pierced in both?"
"Twain gave I to the hammer, nothing loth."

"But surely, Lord, my feet need not be nailed?"
"Had Mine not been, then love had not prevailed."

"What need I more, O Lord, to fill my part?"
"Only the spear-point in a broken heart."

FREDERICK GEORGE SCOTT

IMMUNITY

Think you to escape
What mortal man can never be without?
What saint upon earth has ever lived apart from cross and
    care?
Why, even Jesus Christ, our Lord, was not even for one
    hour free from His passion's pain.
Christ says, "He needs must suffer,
Rising from the dead,
And enter thus upon His glory."
And how do *you* ask for another road
Than this—the Royal Pathway of the Holy Cross.

THOMAS À KEMPIS

JESUS THE CARPENTER

If I could hold within my hand
    The hammer Jesus swung,
Not all the gold in all the land,
Nor jewels countless as the sand,
    All in the balance flung,
Could weigh the value of that thing
Round which His fingers once did cling.

If I could have the table Christ
    Once made in Nazareth,
Not all the pearls in all the sea,
Nor crowns of kings or kings to be
    As long as men have breath,

Could buy that thing of wood He made—
The Lord of Lords who learned a trade.

Yea, but His hammer still is shown
　　By honest hands that toil,
And round His table men sit down;
And all are equals, with a crown
　　Nor gold nor pearls can soil;
The shop of Nazareth was bare—
But brotherhood was builded there.

CHARLES M. SHELDON

THE CHRIST OF COMMON FOLKS

I love the name of Christ the Lord, the Man of Galilee,
Because He came to live and toil among the likes of me.
Let others sing the praises of a mighty King of kings;
I love the Christ of common folks, the Lord of common
　　things.

The beggars and the feeble ones, the poor and sick and blind,
The wayward and the tempted ones, were those He loved
　　to find;
He lived with them to help them like a brother and a
　　friend,
Or like some wandering workman finding things to mend.

I know my Lord is still my kind of folks to this good day;
I know because He never fails to hear me when I pray.
He loves the people that He finds in narrow dingy streets,
And brings a word of comfort to the weary one He meets.

My job is just a poor man's job, my home is just a shack,
But on my humble residence He has never turned His back.
Let others sing their praises to a mighty King of kings;
I love the Christ of common folks, the Lord of common
    things.

GEORGE T. LIDDELL

VISION

We by no shining Galilean lake
Have toiled, but long and little fruitfully
In waves of a more old and bitter sea
Our nets we cast; large winds, that sleep and wake
Around the feet of dawn and sunset, make
Our spiritual inhuman company,
And formless shadows of water rise and flee,
All night around us till the morning break.

Thus our lives wear—shall it be ever thus?
Some idle day, when least we look for grace,
Shall we see stand upon the shore indeed
The visible Master, and the Lord of us,
And leave our nets, nor question of His creed,
Following the Christ within a young man's face?

EDWARD DOWDEN

SIMON'S BURDEN

Compel me, Lord, to bear Thy cross!
   Then, though the weary flesh rebel,
In every hour of pain and loss,
   Thy willing soul shall cry, 'Tis well.

Compel me, Lord, to bear Thy cross,
  Not hermit-like removed from ken,
With fast, and scourge, and bed of moss,
  But in the scornful eyes of men.

Compel me, Lord, to bear Thy cross,
  Remembering Thou wast born for me;
To count the gains of earth as loss,
  And turn from all its smiles to Thee.

Oh, blest Cyrenian! humbly bowed
  Beneath the weight of sinless shame;
Compelled by that infuriate crowd
  To bear reproach for Jesus' name.

So would I walk, not bent with care,
  Nor crushed to earth by heavy dross;
Be mine the helpless, hopeful prayer,
  Compel me, Lord, to bear Thy cross.

ROSE TERRY

FISHERS

Tangled in nets
Of our wild philosophy,
Caught in the backlash
Of ideas ill-cast,
Heaving the lead
Into unplumbed infinity,
Baffled, we stand
Beside the shore at last.

Snagged barbs, snarled lines,
Torn sails! What fishers we!
Teach us thy skill
O Man of Galilee.

ALBERT REGINALD GOLD

IN THE WAY OF PEACE

Jesus, whose love rekindles dying fires
    Flickering to ashes in our aching hearts,
Be Thou the goal of all our best desires,
    The dawn from which our longing ne'er departs.

When night's grim loneliness throbs like a wound,
    And day's bright sunshine stabs us like a sword,
Us, with Thy peace, like traveler's cloak, around,
    Enfold as we go forward, O our Lord.

Through the sharp thorns that lie along our way
    Make Thou a path for tired and bleeding feet;
And bring us to the wonder of that day
    When Love and Memory in Thee shall meet.

LAUCHLAN MacLEAN WATT

From CHRISTUS

My work is finished; I am strong
In faith, and hope, and charity;
For I have written the things I see,
The things that have been and shall be,

Conscious of right, nor fearing wrong;
Because I am in love with Love,
And the sole thing I hate is Hate;
For Hate is death; and Love is life,
A peace, a splendor from above;
And Hate, a never-ending strife,
A smoke, a blackness from the abyss
Where unclean serpents coil and hiss!
Love is the Holy Ghost within;
Hate the unpardonable sin!
Who preaches otherwise than this,
Betrays his Master with a kiss!

HENRY WADSWORTH LONGFELLOW

JESUS

Jesus, whose lot with us was cast,
Who saw it out, from first to last:
Patient and fearless, tender, true,
Carpenter, vagabond, felon, Jew:
Whose humorous eye took in each phase
Of full, rich life this world displays,
Yet evermore kept fast in view
The far-off goal it leads us to:
Who, as Your hour neared, did not fail—
The world's fate trembling in the scale—
With Your half-hearted band to dine,
And chat across the bread and wine:
Then went out firm to face the end,
Alone, without a single friend:
Who felt, as your last words confessed,
Wrung from a proud unflinching breast

By hours of dull ignoble pain,
Your whole life's fight was fought in vain:
Would I could win and keep and feel
That heart of love, that spirit of steel.

Author Unknown

INDEX OF AUTHORS

INDEX OF TITLES

INDEX OF FIRST LINES

ACKNOWLEDGMENTS

The compiler has made every effort to trace the owner-ship of all copyrighted poems. To the best of his knowledge he has secured all necessary permission from authors or their authorized agent, or from both. Should there prove to be any question regarding the use of any poem, the compiler herewith expresses regret for such unconscious error. He will be pleased, upon notification of such error, to make proper acknowledgment in future editions of this book.

Thanks are due the following publishers for permission to use in this anthology the poems indicated:

Charles Scribner's Sons: Poems from the works of Henry van Dyke, Sidney Lanier, John Hall Wheelock, Maltbie D. Babcock, Maxwell Struthers Burt, Alice Maynell and Anna Reeve Aldrich.

Harper & Brothers: "Simon the Cyrenian Speaks" by Countee Cullen, from his volume *Color*.

T. Y. Crowell Company: Poems by Katharine Lee Bates.

Dodd, Mead & Company: "Lord of My Heart's Elation" by Bliss Carman and "The Second Christmas" by Richard Le Gallienne.

Doubleday, Doran & Company: Poems by G. A. Studdert Kennedy, John Oxenham, Joyce Kilmer, Don Marquis ("The Nobler Lesson" from the volume *Dreams and Dust*), Amelia J. Burr and Lizette Woodworth Reese.

Bigelow, Brown & Company: Poems by Oscar Wilde.

W. B. Conkey Company: "Brotherhood" by Ella

Wheeler Wilcox, from her volume *Picked Poems*, and "Gethsemane" and "The Universal Language" by the same author, from the volume, *Poems of Power*.

Fleming H. Revell Company: "How He Came" by William J. Dawson.

Little, Brown & Company: "Christ Has Arisen" by Susan Coolidge.

Methodist Book Concern: "A Man and God" by John T. McFarland.

The Woman's Press: "My Master" by Harry Lee; "My Yoke Is Easy" by Gladys Latchaw, and "Consolator" by Mai Elmendorf Lillie, all reprinted from the volume, *Christ in the Poetry of Today*.

Evangelical Publishers: "Jesus Christ—And We" by Annie Johnson Flint: Reprinted by special permission of the publishers and copyrighters, The Evangelical Publishers, Toronto, Canada.

Brentano's: Poems by Harry Kemp.

L. C. Page Company: "The New Patriot" by Frederick Lawrence Knowles. Copyright is owned by L. C. Page Company, and the poem is used by special permission.

Bobbs Merrill Company: "From Bethlehem to Calvary" by Meredith Nicholson.

Meigs Publishing Company: "Others" by Charles D. Meigs.

Thomas Bird Mosher: "Simon the Cyrenian" by Lucy Lyttelton; "According to St. Mark" by Thomas S. Jones, Jr., from his volume, *Sonnets of the Cross*.

Houghton Mifflin Company: Poems by Henry Wadsworth Longfellow, James Russell Lowell, John Greenleaf Whittier, Richard Watson Gilder and John Drinkwater. These poems are used by permission of and by special arrangement with the publishers.

The Macmillan Company: Poems by Alfred Tennyson, Robert Browning, Christina Rossetti, Thomas Edward Browne and Matthew Arnold. Used by special permission.

Acknowledgment is made also to the following magazines for permission to use the poems indicated:

The Christian Advocate: "Resurrection" and "Undefeated" by Ralph S. Cushman; "The Rhythm of His Life" by Mary Hallet and "An Olive Tree Speaks" by Madeleine Sweeny Miller.

The Boston Transcript: "Had Christ Not Lived and Died" by Edith Lynwood Linn.

The Living Church: "The Potion" by Winnie Lynch Rockett, and "The Rich Young Man" by Laura Simmons.

The Congregationalist: "The Housewife" by Catherine Cate Coblentz.

The Presbyterian Advance: "The Cup" by Frederick T. Roberts.

The Westminster Record: "Prayer Hymn" by M. K. H.

The Christian World: "The Man Christ" by Therese Lindsay; "Beauty" by A. L. C.; "The Password" by Reginald C. Eva; and "In the Way of Peace" by Lauchlan MacLean Watt.

Extension Magazine: "The Splendid Lover" by John Richard Moreland.

The Christian Century: Poems by W. Russell Bowie, Charles G. Blanden, Winfred Ernest Garrison, Daisy Conway Price, Raymond Kresensky, Natalie Flohr, William L. Stidger, Marie LeNart, Arthur R. Macdougall, Jr., Alexander Harvey, Eva Warner, Albert R. Gold, Charles Granville Hamilton, Dwight Bradley, Thomas Curtis Clark, Myriam Page, Mildred Fowler Field, Catherine Williams Herzel, J. N. Scholes, Edgar Daniel Kramer,

Harry Webb Farrington, Gertrude du Bois, Laura Simmons, Churchill Murray, John Richard Moreland, Howard McKinley Corning, Catherine Cate Coblentz, Miriam LeFevre Crouse, Helen Purcell Roads, Mollie Anderson Halen, Edith Mirick, Rex Boundy, Mabel Munns Charles, Aubert Edgar Bruce, Earl Marlatt, Katharine Lee Bates, W. J. Suckow, Marguerite Wilkinson, Hildegarde Hoyt Swift, Carl Vinton Herron, Stella Fisher Burgess, Nellie Knight, Louise Webster, E. McNeill Poteat, Jr., Mary Sinton Leitch, Edward Shillito, Irene McKeighan, Crawford Trotter and George W. Carlin.

The Christian: "I Am the Cross" by William L. Stidger; "Certainties" by Kenneth W. Porter; "The White Presence" by Joseph Fort Newton; "Is This the Time to Halt?" by Charles Sumner Hoyt.

Unity: "To a Student" by E. K. Biddle.

The Churchman: "A River of Grace" by Molly Anderson Haley.

The British Weekly: "Surrender" by Henry W. Clark.

The Personalist: "Resurgam" by John Richard Moreland (also the Irene Leache Memorial, Norfolk, Va., for the poem "Symbols" by J. R. Moreland).

The Lantern: "Sandals" by Gladys Capers Smith.

The Ladies Home Journal: "The Deathless Tale" by Charles Hanson Towne.

The Chicago Tribune: "The World's Lone Lover" by J. R. Perkins.

Harper's Magazine: "The Sepulchre in the Garden" by John Finley.

Messenger of the Sacred Heart Magazine: "And Christ Is Crucified" by John Richard Moreland.

The Classmate: "The Spirit of Youth" and "Who Will Build the World Anew?" by Thomas Curtis Clark.

Special thanks are due also to the following poets, who gave personal permission for the reprinting of selections from their work in this anthology: Edwin Markham, for the use of five poems from his *Collected Poems* copyrighted by Edwin Markham and used by his special permission; Meredith Nicholson, Sarah Cleghorn, Clinton Scollard, John Richard Moreland, Richard Le Gallienne, Laura Simmons, Elias Liebermann, Caroline Hazard, Marie LeNart, Richard Burton, Harry Kemp, Daniel Henderson, Winfred Ernest Garrison, Joseph Fort Newton, Don Marquis, Lucia Trent, Ralph Cheyney, Robert Whitaker, Mary Hallet, John Finley, Daniel Henderson, Henry van Dyke, Frank Mason North, Vida D. Scudder, Charles Buxton Going, Margaret Wade Deland, Charles Hanson Towne, Madeleine Sweeny Miller, Sara Bard Field, Winnie Lynch Rockett, David Morton, Ralph S. Cushman, Gladys Capers Smith, Charlotte Perkins Gilman, Robert Freeman, Raymond Kresensky, Charles G. Blanden, J. R. Perkins, Kenneth W. Porter, Thomas S. Jones, Jr., and E. G. Reith. (Also Dr. Francis Litz for permission to use poems of John B. Tabb; Mrs. Lyman Whitney Allen for permission to use "The Coming of His Feet" by Lyman Whitney Allen, and the estate of Katharine Lee Bates, for permission to use poems of Katharine Lee Bates.)

THE COMPILER